This amazing sto... left off as it chronicles the best beginning to a career that any coach could hope for. The first four years of Johnny Carter's Hall of Fame coaching career is brought back to life in great detail. It takes basketball back to a time when family, team, and community were everything.

    Rick Sherley, Executive Director, TABC
    Texas Association of Basketball Coaches
    Sugar Land, Texas

* * * * *

Coach Leon Black

The Pressing Champions is a great read...especially for coaches looking for ways to maximize their team's chances for winning championships! It gives you a complete understanding of how firm your commitment must be through the process. It is also a great "feel good" story of a coach's love of family, players, community, and God. A winning formula in any field!

    Coach Leon Black
    Retired men's basketball coach
    University of Texas at Austin 1967-1976

* * * * *

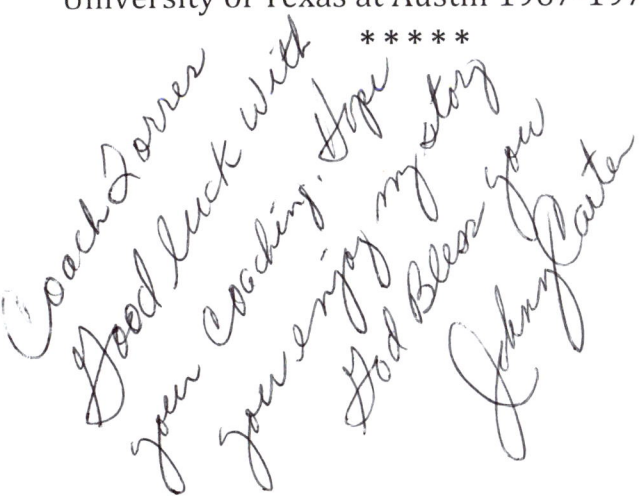

Coach Billy Tubbs

A truly amazing beginning for a very young coach. The story demonstrates how changing to a continuous full-court pressure defense allowed this team to not only compete, but usually defeat much larger teams.

Billy Tubbs
Retired head coach Lamar University,
Oklahoma University, TCU

* * * * *

Daniel J. Kaspar

As a junior college player at McLennan Community College in 1974-75, I learned a great deal about full and ¾ court presses from Coach Johnny Carter. My high school team pressed infrequently and my knowledge of this aspect of the game was somewhat limited. Coach Carter changed that and expanded my views on how to attack defensively. Our MCC team would often revert to the full and/or ¾ court press to change/disrupt the flow of the game to our advantage. We won many games using these various defensive presses and they deserve great credit for our Conference title, 27-5 record, and our advancement to the regional finals where we lost a hard-fought game to the eventual National Champion that year.

Coach Carter did a great job in going into detail about the fundamentals of executing a proper trap, the spacing of defenders in the various presses we ran, pressing without fouling, communication in the press, and recovering back to your ½ court defense if the press is beaten in a manner that minimizes easy baskets by the offense. As a collegiate coach, I can attest that Coach Carter's book would be a great help to teams lacking size, but possessing quickness, speed, and good anticipation abilities. It certainly helped our MCC team in 1975 and helped me in my coaching career a great deal!

Danny Kaspar
MCC-1975
Head Men's Basketball Coach
Texas State University

* * * * *

Vinnie "The Microwave" Johnson

Coach Carter helped me bridge the gap from the playground to the NBA.

—Vinnie "The Microwave" Johnson
Detroit Pistons NBA champions 1989, 1990

* * * * *

Sam Worthen

Coach Carter helped me prepare for life with lessons from the basketball court.

—Sam Worthen
Chicago Bulls, Washington Generals
Harlem Globetrotters

Tony Maudlin

Coach Johnny Carter was my mentor and my model for an aggressive pressing coaching style. I first became associated with Coach Carter at Howard Payne College (now Howard Payne University) where I was a player and he was the Assistant Coach. Playing under Coach Carter I came to realize that a full commitment to pressing, not only during games but also conditioning, practice, and drills, was the model I wanted to copy as I began my career in coaching.

Coach Carter's second book explains the press as I knew and learned from him. The pressing style of play described in Coach Carter's book is what I used to win over 800 games, be inducted into the Texas Basketball Hall of Fame, and named National High School Coach of the Year. Due to what I learned from Coach Carter, I had the career that I had. Thank you, Coach!

*****

Rodney Terry

A coach can control the preparation and effort daily with each practice which leads to every game. The opportunity for success is usually disguised as hard work. This book is all about the importance of sound fundamental defense and the impact it has from game to game. I highly recommend *The Pressing Champions* and think you will enjoy reading it.

Head basketball coach
University of Texas, El Paso

Thomas Poe

Recently, I had lunch with the Carter boys. Each one has been very successful in their own profession: Billy (law), James Otis or Ottie to his friends (business), and Johnny (education). Mary Frank and John Dean Carter were proud of their boys and instilled in them a competitive spirit and sense of fair play which served them well both on and off the basketball court.

Mr. and Mrs. Carter also taught their boys that everyone should be treated with dignity and respect, which is a trademark of the Carter family. Johnny's two books have chronicled the lives of a unique and talented Coach and the young men who executed to perfection his full court press and fast-break offense.

Thomas Poe
Teammate Madisonville Mustangs, 1961

* * * * *

Vern Lewis

My dad, Coach Guy V. Lewis and I really loved Coach Carter's first book, *The First Season.*

This second book, *The Pressing Champions,* is a continuation of that book and goes into detail about the radical change that a young coach made in his approach to the game. Continuous full-court pressure defense was a style of play that hardly anyone used at that time and though knowing very little about it, he carefully and successfully implemented this with his team. I highly recommend this book.

—Vern Lewis

Carroll Dawson

I grew up in a small town in East Texas, so I have no trouble identifying with this story. Most small schools always seemed to be short on funds, teachers, equipment and facilities. Kennard High School was no exception.

When Johnny Carter's young team surprised everyone and won the state championship in his first year to coach, it might be considered a miracle.

Changing his team's style of play in the second year and employing a start-to-finish full court press defense, he had many of his most ardent supporters scratching their heads. With a lot of patience, he strategically sold his players on the importance of great defense and after many victories soon convinced the fans as well. Not only did his team win a lot of games, this new pressing defense propelled them to a second consecutive state championship and later, a third title.

Now success is well and good, but most people don't realize the discipline, determination, togetherness, teamwork, plus the many long hours of practice that it takes to mold a special team. A lot of character-building is involved in the process of helping prepare each player for a productive future. This special story is what dreams are made of and I think you will enjoy reading it.

—Carroll Dawson
Former NBA Coach and Executive
Houston Rockets

Herman Myers

When Coach Carter was hired to coach the Kennard Tigers, we were excited to have a young coach who had actually played college basketball. Our first impression was that he was humble and likable, but seemed too shy to be a good coach…that is, until he walked into the gym. His reserve was gone and that shyness was nowhere to be seen.

It quickly became obvious that he not only knew the game, but how to teach us how to play at a much higher level. When mistakes were pointed out, it was done in a way that wasn't taken personally.

Coach Carter was constantly stressing teamwork and togetherness, while showing respect for each player, as well as our administrators, teachers, other teams, referees, and the fans.

What a blessing it was to live every player's dream and play on not one, but two state championship teams. It's hard to believe that it's been 50 years since this took place and that special memory will never go away. The most impressive thing about this incredible experience is that the friendships that developed among our players remains to this day.

—Herman Myers
Kennard point guard 1968
* * * * *

Craig Smoak

Coming from New York City as the first out-of-state player at McLennan Community College in Waco, Texas, I thought I was a pretty good basketball player. I was then introduced to Coach Carter's eye-opening, continuous full-court pressure defense. This added a new dimension to my overall game, thus allowing me to refine and improve my skills.

Coach Carter's personality and coaching style was infectious. He and I became more than just coach and player, but the closest of friends and that special friendship remains to this day.

—Craig Smoak
San Antonio, Texas

The Pressing Champions

Coach Johnny Carter

COPYRIGHT

The Pressing Champions
Copyright ©2018 by Johnny Carter

All rights reserved. No part of this book may be used or reproduced in any manner without written permission, except in the case of brief quotations embodied in critical articles or reviews.

ISBN-13: 978-1985584648
ISBN-10: 1985584646

Printed in the United States of America

For more information, please visit
CoachJohnnyCarter.com

SPECIAL THANKS

Thanks, Mom and Dad
Without your love, backing, and guidance,
none of these special memories in this book would
have been made for all of us.

DEDICATION

*I can do all things through Christ
which strengthened me.
— Philippians 4:13*

I dedicate this book to all of the young men who played on my teams at Kennard High School from 1967–1970, three of those years in which we won the state championship. You all gave it everything you had, every game. You never gave up. You made me, your teammates, your families, the Kennard community, and, most importantly, yourselves proud.

Thank you for the memories that are shared by all of us.

TABLE OF CONTENTS

The Texas State Basketball Tournament	vii
Prologue	ix
Foreword	xi
Chapter 1: "Only Hamburgers"	1
Chapter 2: "Everyone Has An Opinion"	11
Chapter 3: "Here Comes the Press"	27
Chapter 4: "Never Enough Practice"	35
Chapter 5: "A New Look"	42
Chapter 6: "The Second Season"	44
Chapter 7: "Snook"	60
Chapter 8: "Cheat Toward the Ball"	74
Chapter 9: "Cayuga"	85
Chapter 10: "The Playoffs"	88
Chapter 11: "The Regional Tournament"	92
Chapter 12: "The Regional Finals"	101
Chapter 13: ""Saved by a Sophomore"	107
Chapter 14: "Austin, here we are again!"	117
Chapter 15: "State '68"	120
Chapter 16: "State Final 1968"	132
Chapter 17: "An Earned Miracle"	146
Chapter 18: "Everyone Wants a Winning Team:	169
Chapter 19: "Tragedy"	173
Chapter 20: "Another Year"	175
Chapter 21: "Inexperience"	183
Chapter 22: "The Challenging District Race"	191
Chapter 23: "A Heartbreaking Loss"	197
Chapter 24: "Swarm of Bees"	204
Chapter 25: "First Saturday in June:	213
Chapter 26: "You Did Not Run Back HARD!"	220
Chapter 27: "Total Team Togetherness"	228
Chapter 28: "Going Home"	238
Chapter 29: ""Any Friends Left?"	253
Chapter 30: "Diboll Again!"	258

TABLE OF CONTENTS [cont.]

Chapter 31: "The Playoffs"	274
Chapter 32: "The Regional Tournament"	288
Chapter 33: "State Tournament Again"	307
Chapter 34: "State Championship Game At Last!"	330
Photos	351
About the Author	358
Acknowledgments	361
Praise for *The Pressing Champions*	364

THE TEXAS STATE BASKETBALL TOURNAMENT

The Texas State Basketball Tournament has an amazing history going back over ninety years.

Indeed, during that time Coach M.N. "Cotton" Robinson's legacy of seven state championships at Buna High School stands out among all the others. From the small community of Leona, Texas, Coach Robinson credits his high school coach, Bill Bitner, as the most influential person in his life.

Growing up in Madisonville, just ten miles south of Leona, Johnny Carter graduated in 1961. His Mustang team faced Buna that year in the regional finals, losing a close game to Coach Robinson's undefeated squad.

Ironically, five years later, Carter was sent to Kennard High School for his first coaching job by none other than Bill Bitner. Carter would win three state championships in his four years there. Coach Carter's heartwarming story of the miracle that was *The First Season*" now continues with his second book, *The Pressing Champions.*

PROLOGUE
Kennard, Texas

Kennard is located in the Pinetree country of East Texas about 30 miles west of Lufkin and 16 miles east of Crockett in Houston County. In 1899, this town was established when a small sawmill began operation some four miles west of the present-day community of Ratcliff. It was called the Four C Mill and as its size and productivity increased, a settlement developed near the mill.

Founded in 1901, Kennard grew rapidly with the expansion of the mill which would become the largest sawmill west of the Mississippi. With its growth, expansion, and productivity, the lumber company established a much-needed short railroad line between Kennard and Lufkin. The Eastern Texas Railroad Company serviced the mill transporting its timber. Many seeking employment migrated to the Kennard/Ratcliff communities, actually spiraling the population of Ratcliff to well over 5,000.

Air circulation at the mill was a problem. In the summer of 1909, workers began the installation of a "cool air system." Although it's not clear what type of cooling system this was, it was said to be the first air-conditioning unit in the state of Texas.

The area's lumbering industry thrived for many years, but by 1920 it had deforested over 120,000 acres. With the depletion of virtually all the timber, the mill was forced to shut down. This was the beginning of a major decline in the population of both Kennard and Ratcliff.

The Civilian Conservation Corps saved the landscape by planting over three million trees in the 1930s and it became part of the Davy Crockett National Forest. The 45-acre pond used by the lumbering operation would become Ratcliff Lake, evolving into a recreational area, campground, and tourist attraction. As the population of Ratcliff continued to decline, its schools consolidated with the Kennard Common School District in 1955.

The town of Kennard was incorporated in 1969 and the school became an ISD in 1974. This is a relatively poor community with the average median income less than half of the state's over-all average. In the year 2000, the population of Kennard was 317 while Ratcliff was at 106. The area's population has not fluctuated very much since then. Our story goes back in time and begins in March of 1967.

FOREWORD

Coach Johnny Carter had a slam dunk with his first book, *The First Season*. That book was an outstanding story of his very first year in coaching. Remarkably, as a twenty-three-year-old head coach, he led his team to a Texas high school state championship!

Coach Carter is back with another book, *The Pressing Champions*. This one focuses on not only another state title, but an undefeated state championship team as well. It appears that Coach Carter not only had the magic when it came to coaching, but he has saved some of that magic dust for another great book on high school basketball.

The emphasis on a pressing defense is a key component in this story. Coach Carter had undersized teams at Kennard High School. He was not going to consistently beat opponents playing half-court defense. His teams would have been good, but not great. Most likely, they would not have won a second state title. They certainly would not have been undefeated.

Many teams during the era of the 1960s and 1970s won by simply pounding the ball into the post on offense and playing solid man-to-man or zone defense in the half court. That was precisely the recipe Coach Carter utilized to win the 1967 state title.

Very few coaches utilized the full court press or the fast break. Breaking from the norm was a courageous move for a young coach. Making the decision to make a drastic change in philosophy was a difficult chore. He would have to convince his players and his fans that this was the best option. He would also have to convince himself.

This courageous and brilliant move was the difference in his second championship in 1968. The pressing defense used by Coach Carter and the Kennard Tigers separated his team from all others.

Significantly, the pressing defense was symbolic to Coach Carter, his team, the parents, and the community who supported them. Pressing was emblematic of the way they lived their lives. Moving forward each day. Giving one's best no matter the circumstances. Not backing down from challenges. Never being afraid. Attacking the game of life. Never being satisfied with a previous success. Learning to be dependent upon one another. Not allowing others to dictate their destiny or their path to success.

These were all part of the philosophy of a pressing defense. The psychological aspect of a full court pressure defense plays havoc on opponents. Most coaches dread the aspect of playing against teams who use pressure defense. Talented teams can be pressed effectively because most other teams are afraid to press the good teams. The Kennard Tigers pressed everyone and they did so the entire game. They used the pressing defense as both a psychological ally as well as a physical weapon.

Keep in mind full court pressure defense requires great physical conditioning. A coach who employs this style of play must either have a long bench with multiple substitutes or he has to get his team in top-notch condition, physically and mentally. Coach Carter chose a highly disciplined form of conditioning for his team. He did not have the luxury of a deep bench.

He knew that his players risked getting into foul trouble when pressing full court. He also knew that there would be injuries and fatigue. However, he also recognized the heart of his players. He knew this team was willing and able to pay the price in order to become champions—and that they did.

Coach Johnny Carter pressed right into another state championship. He utilized his own strong personality, his love for his players, and their love for one another. He met every one who doubted his ability and his strategy with the same outlook. He pressed on!

Having utilized the full court press in my own coaching career, I can attest to the value of this defensive strategy. The last team I coached averaged 109.4 points per game. The full court press gives teams that are small in stature the best chance to win. Coach Carter understood this long before I did. He would go on to win another state championship in 1970, giving him three state titles in four years.

Coach Carter was a phenomenal coach at both the high school and collegiate level. His teams were known for their clean yet aggressive play. His accomplishments earned him an induction into the Texas High School Basketball Hall of Fame.

Thus, we have a great Hall of Fame Coach writing on a topic that he believed separated his team from the rest of the pack. *The Pressing Champions* is another great book from a championship coach. I know you will enjoy reading about this coach and his undefeated team.

            Dr. Charles Breithaupt
            University Interscholastic League
            Executive Director
            Austin, Texas

Illustration by my son, John Carter

Chapter 1
Only Hamburgers?

Where do I go from here? I was 23 years old and a first-year coach who had just fulfilled a lifelong dream. My unheralded basketball team from little known Kennard High School had just won the State championship in my very first year.

I had grown up in basketball, taking numerous trips to the Texas state basketball tournament from the time I was in the fifth grade. It was love at first sight, establishing a passion for the sport and a goal in life to play in that very prestigious tournament.

After playing on some very good teams at Madisonville High School, we came real close to getting

Coach Johnny Carter

to Austin, but were denied three straight years by the eventual state champion. This was a heartbreaking experience for me at the time and yet would later be one of the primary reasons that I would change my major at University of Houston from radio/television to become a coach.

When I graduated, my sole purpose in coaching was to take a team to the state tournament, let alone win it. Many coaches I knew had coached for over 40 years had never made it. So, I was expecting that if it happened for me, it would take many years, plus a lot of luck to get it done if at all.

Exiting Gregory Gym that unforgettable day on the University of Texas campus, I was spellbound by what had just taken place. How could this have happened in my very first year of coaching? I was just learning how to coach and we win the state championship! This indeed was a true miracle! I felt totally blessed. Somehow through the grace of the Good Lord my dark horse team from the pine tree country of East Texas had just surprised everyone. We had achieved the impossible.

As I walked down the steps leaving the gym, I thought I was dreaming. Having just celebrated my birthday, I once again looked to the heavens and thanked the Good Lord for walking me through this. I was on Cloud Nine and the feelings inside me were indescribable. There was a bounce in my step and the broad smiles on the young faces of my players said it all.

The Pressing Champions

Honestly, I don't think any of us truly realized at that moment what had just happened and the impact it would have on our lives. With the scent of early spring hovering in the air that delightful March morning, the purple blooms of the Texas mountain laurel not only matched our school colors, but now appeared to be even more brilliant than when we arrived to play in the state championship game.

Upon our arrival at a very nice restaurant, I told my team to order anything they wanted, even though our school was very poor and our funds were limited.

"This is a one-time thing, fellas, so let's make this a very special meal. Every team in the state would love to be in our position right now, so enjoy yourself because this will probably never happen again."

Haywood Henderson, my very athletic wing man, looked up from his menu and with a slight smile said, "At least not until next year."

I smiled as Roy Harrison, my undersized post man, chimed in. "Coach, you better not leave us because we're coming back here again next year."

I smiled again, full knowing that repeating what just happened would be much harder than the first time. Being the underdog had a lot of advantages because no one thought that we would make it to Austin, much less win the state championship. Many teams simply looked at us as a stepping stone to bigger things and took us as an afterthought.

However, next year we will be the favorite in every game. Our opponent will be extra motivated, thus going all out to knock off the defending champion.

Purposely changing the subject, I asked the team, "Do you guys know what you want to eat?"

To my surprise, it was 100% double-meat cheeseburgers. With a surprised look on my face, I said, "You mean to tell me that you guys have a chance to eat anything on the menu and you're choosing hamburgers?"

After a sip of his Dr. Pepper, our best shooter, Herman Myers, had an earnest look on his face when he said, "A good hamburger is my favorite meal."

James "Nubbin" Pilkington, our best defensive man, nodded his head in agreement.

I shook my head and said, "It's your day, your choice. As for me, I'm going to have a nice juicy medium-well steak. "How about you, Fred? You just finished your high school career in style and you owe yourself a steak." Fred Pilkington, our lead-by-example post man and only senior starter looked at me and said, "Sounds good to me."

As we enjoyed a great meal together, I looked into the young faces of our team that had just defied all odds. Only two weeks ago I had my doubts if we could win one playoff game and today we became the state champion. While my team was thrilled at what had just transpired, they were not anywhere as thrilled as I was. I literally was on top of the world! This was not only my dream, it's every coach's dream. I actually felt a little bit guilty that this happened to me at such a young age when so many coaches had worked their entire life trying to achieve what we had just done. However, I wasn't about to give that trophy back. What a special time! What a special moment! What an extra-special birthday present! It just doesn't get any better than this!

Austin was soon in our rearview mirror as we headed down the road back to Kennard. There was joy in the air as we were savoring the after-effects of that magnificent magical moment. The Redbud trees, which were barely noticeable on the way to Austin, now lit up the landscape as their radiant pink blooms were bursting with beauty. Actually, when you're coming back from the state tournament after winning, everything seems beautiful!

Soon we were on the outskirts of Madisonville and stopped to visit with my parents. They were enjoying all this, maybe even more than I was, if that was possible. Congratulations were in order as my dad shook hands with every player on our team. He was all smiles, loving this moment.

Mom, on the other hand, as she always did, offered everyone a slice of fresh-baked cake and a bag of cookies for each player to take home with them.

My dad was all smiles as he addressed our group.

"When Johnny was born, I told my wife that one day he would do something very special. I had no idea that it would come at such an early age. This is one of the proudest moments of my life and I want to thank every one of you for helping make a wonderful memory."

There was a sweet aroma emerging from the kitchen as Mom opened her oven. Herman looked at Mom with a big smile. "Are you baking one of those pound cakes?"

She looked at Herman smiling and responded, "It brought you guys good luck for the tournament and now I want it to bring you good luck next year."

"Thank you, Mrs. Carter, but I really think that I'm the lucky one...not next year, but right now because I can't wait to have a piece of that warm pound cake!"

Now everyone was laughing, particularly Gary Parrish, my sixth man, and Lester Hutcherson, the only freshman on the team. My parents were truly the unsung heroes in the background for our team's success and I made sure that every player thanked them for their support.

We were soon on the road again, cruising down Highway 21 East, passing over the Trinity River, through Crockett, and finally down Highway 7. You know you're almost home when all you can see are pine trees stretching toward the sky and at this time of the year the soft, serene, statuesque beauty of blooming dogwoods at their base.

Soon we were approaching Kennard, a small logging community nestled right in the middle of the Davy Crockett National Forest. Even though I knew what was about to happen, my players had no clue. They were in for yet another huge surprise. As we approached the school parking lot, we noticed cars everywhere. Nubbin looked at me, scratched his head and said, "What's this all about?"

I just shrugged my shoulders, giving the impression that I had no idea.

As we entered the gym, we were totally amazed. The stands were packed with ecstatic, enthusiastic fans. The cheerleaders were there in their uniforms.

With megaphone in hand, Gwen Parrish shouted, "Let's hear it for the 1967 state champions!" Soon we were receiving a long-standing ovation which evolved into a riotous riveting of the rafters in our soon-to-be-perfect-for-the-press gym. My surprised players were simply blown away by this reception and though thrilled at how this season ended, obviously our fans did not want all of this to be over!

Gwen then turned to me and said, "Coach, we need a speech!"

I shook my head side to side, giving the impression that I didn't want to make a speech, but then the massive crowd erupted again, shouting in unison, "Speech! Speech! Speech!"

Reluctantly, I went to the microphone. Not really knowing what to say, I nervously began to speak.

"Thank you for being here and all of your support. This is such a unique occasion and I am honored to be the coach of this special team."

Gesturing toward my players, I continued. "Look, this isn't about me, it's about these guys."

With that, the crowd erupted again with a lengthy, unified, heart-filled ovation. Resembling the after-effects of an earthquake, the walls were shaking, releasing a fine mist of dust from the ceiling. When the crowd noise finally died down, I spoke again.

"There are so many people I want to thank, but first and foremost, the Good Lord because without Him none of this would've happened.

I'd like to thank Mr. Bitner for hiring me and giving me a chance, Mr. Phillips and all of the teachers, in particular, Mr. Frizzell, all the cafeteria ladies, especially Miss Nona, her son, Curtis, our cheerleaders, students and parents."

I then gestured again toward my team. "Last, but certainly not least, our newly crowned state champions!"

I didn't even have a chance to thank them when this massive crowd again erupted with an enthusiastic chant of approval that was so loud that the hair on the back of my neck stood up.

As I left the gym and headed to my car in the parking lot, I heard, "Wait up, Coach! I'd like to talk to you for a second."

It was Bob Currie, a local bulldozing contractor and one of our biggest supporters.

"I just want to offer my congratulations on one incredibly great season. You did something with this team that nobody around here, including me, thought was possible."

"Thanks, Bob, I appreciate that. We had some great team chemistry and these guys really take to coaching well. I feel blessed being here."

He smiled and then his expression became serious. "Actually, Coach, this town, this community, and in particular, this school...we're all blessed to have you here. If I can ever do anything to help you, just give me a call."

It was early evening and even though I was physically, mentally, and emotionally exhausted, I decided to drive to Madisonville to spend the rest of the weekend with my family. We'd played three straight early-morning games in Austin, which meant having to get up very early to eat our pre-game breakfast. This early morning acclimation in adjusting to our schedule had me really looking forward to sleeping in.

The game to game constant intense pressure of playoff basketball had done a number on me. Literally not knowing if each game might be your last can be very nerve-wracking. I was relieved that it was finally over.

My parents had already retired for the evening before I got home. It didn't take me long to fall sound asleep.

When I woke up the next morning, I was totally disoriented and thought I was still in Austin with one

Coach Johnny Carter

more game to play. I rushed into the kitchen where Mom was cooking breakfast. In a panic, I said, "Mom, we've got to wake those guys up! We've got a game in thirty minutes!"

She looked at me like I was crazy and laughed.

"Son, you must be sleep-walking. You won the state championship yesterday. This is Sunday. Go back to bed."

Finally, I regained my wits, smiled at Mom, and then headed back to bed.

Chapter 2
Everyone has an Opinion

Later that afternoon, after a Sunday morning service at the First Methodist Church, I was visiting with my two brothers, Billy and James Otis.

Billy, a member of the Rice University basketball team, looked at me and with a big smile said, "Well, how does it feel to finally be part of a state championship team?"

"Well, you and I both know what it's like to get to the regional finals and be denied that trip to Austin by the team that would win it all. This erases all of that past frustration and boy it does feel great, but I hate to think what our fans are going to expect from me next year."

"Well, Johnny, since you have four starters returning, if you don't win it all next year, it's going to be a bad year."

"Thanks a lot, Billy! Just what I needed to hear," I sarcastically replied.

James Otis, now a senior at Madisonville High School added, "Like it or not, a lot of people are going to think that it was just beginner's luck, so you definitely have your work cut out for you next year."

"Would you guys let me just enjoy what happened? I'll worry about next year when it rolls around. Besides, I have some big changes in mind that I'm thinking about employing next year. You guys know that I don't have a real positive feeling about the zone defense. I know that's what we used as our main defense this year and I have to admit that it worked really well for us. However, I know in my heart that man-to-man defense is what I want to do.

"Look, I realize that changing from zone to man is much more difficult than vice versa, so I know that I'm going to have to really work hard on teaching the fundamentals of man defense. What do you guys think?"

Billy gave me a surprised look. "It's much harder to teach, but I agree it's a better defense."

I gave him a serious look. "That's not the only change I plan on making. I'm thinking about going to an all-out, in-your-face full-court press, start to finish incorporating both zone and man principles."

With a concerned look on his face, James Otis said, "Let me get this straight. This year you won the state championship using a zone defense and now you want to go straight man? You also basically played a pretty conservative half-court offense and now you're going to open it up with a much faster style of play? You know, if that doesn't work, there will be a whole lot of criticism."

"I know, but the fast-paced style of play fits me like a glove. You saw how well we responded using the full-court press in the last quarter of the regional final. It was the main reason we came from way behind and got to go to the state tournament in the first place.

The Pressing Champions

"I love the idea that your opponent has to earn every inch of the floor to get to the basket. I also know that hardly anyone presses the whole game nowadays, but I think it's something that will work. Besides, if it works the way I think it will, our defense will become a major part of our offense. This will be an aggressive style of play that I think our players will love and it should be very exciting for the fans. The hard part is to convince our players that it will work. You have to sell them."

Billy looked at me and smiled. "That's where coaching comes into play."

Illustration by my son, John Carter

Coach Johnny Carter

It was early Monday morning. I walked down the deserted hallway headed toward the school cafeteria. Nona Baker and her son, Curtis were seated at a table.

When she saw me, Nona said, "Have a seat, Coach. I'll get your cup of coffee."

Curtis, who had been extremely helpful to our team with his insight and scouting, took a sip of coffee and smiled at me. "How does it feel to win the state championship in your very first season?"

"I'm blessed, Curtis. You know as well as I do that this probably should never have happened. I'm just learning how to coach and we win the state championship. Come on! I really think the Good Lord walked me through the whole thing. I don't think my players knew exactly how nervous I truly was, particularly in the regional final in Kilgore."

"You're a pretty good actor, Coach, because you definitely fooled your players. Heck, you even fooled me!"

"Well, let's just keep that between you and me."

Upon hearing the end of our conversation, Nona smiled, handed me a cup of coffee and one of her delicious apricot fried pies.

"Our lips are sealed, Coach."

I gave Nona a big smile. "You know, I've enjoyed your fried pies all year and they've always tasted great, but I believe today's is the best tasting one you've made all year!"

The Pressing Champions

She laughed, then said, "This one is no different than all the others, but then you hadn't won the state championship when you ate all the others."

All three of us were laughing big time as the first period bell rang. I was heading out the door when Nona stopped me.

"Hang on, Coach, I've got something to tell you. I want to thank you and your team for single-handedly helping us get through this first year of integration with few problems. You just don't realize the impact y'all had on our little community. I want to personally thank you for that."

"Thank you, Nona, but I think you're over-estimating that just a tad."

"No, I'm not! I've seen it firsthand over and over and again!" She gave me a big hug. "Thanks again, Coach."

I was humbled and mildly surprised. I gave her an appreciative smile and headed to class.

There was one small café in Kennard. Thrilled by what our team had accomplished, we were invited to a dinner by the owners. It was an enjoyable meal and a grand time was had by all, with a lot of reminiscing going on. Our players continued to be impressed with all of the attention they were getting.

Ironically, a couple weeks later, Roy Harrison, one of my black players, ordered a meal at this same café and was told he would have to eat it in the kitchen. Roy didn't let his inner feelings affect the way he reacted because he acted like everything was okay.

"No problem, my aunt is your cook, so I'll eat back there with her."

When I heard this, I was very disappointed. Despite what Miss Nona had previously said about our basketball team starting to bridge the gap with the black and white issue, there obviously was more work to be done. Even though our team had successfully come together with integration, undoubtedly it was going to be more difficult in the community.

Back in December, shortly after Snook defeated us in the Madisonville tournament, I called and secured two games with them for next year. At the time these games were scheduled, Snook was the two-time defending state champion. Two weeks after Snook got upset in the state tournament and we emerged as the state champion, I got a phone call from Coach Jimmy Horn canceling our two games. He claimed he'd checked the map and the distance was just too far. I found that hard to believe, so I tried to convince him that this was an ideal match between two state champions. This would have been two guaranteed standing-room-only crowds and a definite marquee matchup. This irked me, my players, and our fans, but there was nothing I could do about it. I did tell my players that we would have a chance to play them in the Madisonville tournament.

When informed of this cancellation, Curtis said, "I thought that Snook would play anybody, anytime,

The Pressing Champions

anywhere. I just wonder if the fact that we had four juniors returning had anything to do with that decision."

With the school year coming to a close, plans were being made for our athletic banquet. Jerry Phillips, our high school principal, asked me if I had anybody in mind to be the guest speaker.

"You know, I grew up a big SMU fan and I would love to get their head basketball coach, E.O. "Doc" Hayes, as our speaker."

Jerry gave me a skeptical look and said, "Coach, there's no way we're going to get "Doc" Hayes to come to little Kennard, Texas to speak at our banquet. He just won the Southwest Conference championship for the eighth or ninth time and he's in big demand. Your chance of getting him is about the same as it is for us winning the state championship again next year. You better try to get somebody else."

What Jerry didn't realize was that I had some inside on this situation. The coach at Richards High School, Tommy Ferguson, was one of my best friends and we had grown up together as big SMU fans. Tommy's mom had grown up with "Doc" Hayes and knew him well. I called Tommy, he called his mom, she called SMU, the famous SMU coach then called me and bingo, we got him as our guest speaker.

The next morning, I couldn't wait to inform Jerry what had happened. "You're pulling my leg, Coach. "Doc" Hayes called you? Right! Just how did you pull that off?"

Coach Johnny Carter

"Hey, when you compare us winning another state championship next year to getting "Doc" Hayes for our banquet, it's no contest! You know as well as I do that us winning the state championship again next year just might take another miracle."

I couldn't resist a little sarcasm of my own. With raised eyebrows, I said, "However, getting "Doc" Hayes was a piece of cake."

Jerry had a stunned look on his face as I exited his office with a big smile on mine.

Being the only coach at Kennard, I was assigned to coach everything—boys, girls, high school, and junior high. We were now into track season and even though my knowledge of track was limited, I had to do the job. We had a relatively successful season and Fred Pilkington qualified for State in the mile run. Benefiting from all of our running in basketball, not to mention Fred's intensity in this very difficult event, he finished fourth in the state meet. Athletically, Fred just finished an incredible senior year. This humble, lead-by-example young man would definitely be missed next year.

The Pressing Champions

Loyal Fans

Fred Pilkington hits a big shot against Krum, 1967 State championship game

Coach Johnny Carter

Roy Harrison scores against Krum in the state championship game. In the last two minutes he hit three big baskets and with each one our team regained the lead. Thanks Roy!!

The Pressing Champions

1967 Championship Team

Danny Smith, Jerry Parrish, Herman Myers, Gary Parrish, Fred Pilkington, Leeland Strban, Eddie Ray Pilkington, Haywood Henderson, James Pilkington, Roy Harrison, Walter Denman, Lester Hutcherson

Purple Hats after State Final game

Coach Johnny Carter

Fred Pilkington
All District, All Regional
All State Tourney
All State, North – South
All star game

Coach Carter with 1967 trophy

The Pressing Champions

1967 Cheerleaders
(L-R) Nelda Myers, Carolyn Fowler, Mary Davis, Gwen Parrish (Head cheerleader) Judy Hill

Kennard High School Girls Varsity Basketball Team
(L-R) Nelda Myers, Mary Davis, Janice Johnson, Regina Westbrook, Mary Creath, Coach Carter, Helen Connor, Mary Kennedy, Judy Hill, Gwen Parrish, Louise McKinney.

Coach Johnny Carter

**25-year State Tournament Reunion
for 1967 and 1968 State Champions
March 1992**

Top (L-R) Coach Carter, Jerry Parrish, Fred Pilkington, Leeland Strban, Gary Parrish

Bottom (L-R) Herman Myers, Roy Harrison, James Smith, James Pilkington, Lester Hutcherson

The Pressing Champions

THE ROAD TO STATE 1967

Kennard 67	Zavalla 44
Kennard 48	Zavalla 32
Kennard 50	Douglas 34
Kennard 41	Slocum 39
Kennard 61	Slocum 49
Kennard 55	Douglas 57
Kennard 52	Richards 40
Kennard 50	Chireno 43
Kennard 34	Chireno 36
Kennard 64	LaPoyner 52
Kennard 52	Richards 37
Kennard 64	Maydelle 41
Kennard 61	Crockett 47
Kennard 50	Maydelle 25
Kennard 62	Redland 48
Kennard 66	Bryan JV 46
Kennard 53	Trinity 34
Kennard 36	Snook 48
Kennard 55	Fairfield 35
Kennard 67	Neches 46
Kennard 40	Crockett 21
Kennard 51	Trinity 45
Kennard 58	Alto 39
Kennard 42	Richards 32
Kennard 73	Elkhart 33
Kennard 65	Coldspring 49

Coach Johnny Carter

Kennard 69	Rosebud 48
Kennard 67	Neches 62
Kennard 70	Redland 36
Kennard 72	Latexo 45
Kennard 58	Apple Springs 46
Kennard 52	Lovelady 36
Kennard 75	Centerville (Gr.) 52
	Forfeit Latexo
Kennard 62	Redland 48
Kennard 69	Apple Springs 49
Kennard 51	Lovelady 40
Kennard 57	Centerville (Gr.) 53
Kennard 50	Hudson 51
Kennard 44	Grapeland 43
BI-DISTRICT	
Kennard 79	Anderson 55
REGIONAL	
Kennard 71	Frankston 53
Kennard 60	Avinger 59
STATE TOURNAMENT	
Kennard 59	Avoca 47
Kennard 77	Plainview 67 (Washington)
Kennard 51	Krum 47

STATE CHAMPIONS RECORD: 42-4

Chapter 3
Here Comes the Press

During spring basketball practice, I began implementing the full-court pressure defense, even though I didn't know whole lot about it. I knew it was going to be a trial-and-error experience at the beginning because it would be a learning process for both the players and me.

The main problem with teaching that style of play was convincing players the importance of getting back down the floor as quickly as possible when you didn't get a steal. Obviously, your opponent is going to successfully get the ball down the floor many more times than you get turnovers or steals. This fact alone makes being in great shape a prerequisite for the press. So basically, we had to be in much better shape than we were this year. This meant a whole lot more running and conditioning and I wasn't about to let this be a roadblock.

In addressing my players and discussing this plan, I said, "You guys thought I ran you hard this year, well that was just a drop in the bucket compared to what's about to happen next year. The pressing defense is going to become a major part of our game and the only way I'm going to use it is to do it the right way. You thought you were in good shape this year. Next year you're going to be in great shape! So, get your mind focused on this plan because I'm going to work you much harder next year. I want you to be able to play as hard the last minute of the game as you do the first minute. I promise you, we will never lose a game because we're tired. I will personally take care of that. So, get ready. We're going to have a great season next year. Believe me, this new style of play is perfect for our team."

Herman gave me an inquisitive look and said, "Coach, I don't know if I can get in any better shape than I was this year."

With a stern look on my face, I looked at Herman and replied, "You can…and believe me you will. Besides, with this fast-paced game, you're going to get a whole lot more shots than you got this year."

Upon hearing this, the expression on Herman's face changed to a big smile.

"Look, when we had to go to the full-court press in the regional final and came from way back to win that game, that sent a message to me. If we can finish a game with that kind of intensity, then why not start the game the same way?

"The point I want to stress today is that the main objective after we score is to not let them get the ball in. What this means is when the ball goes through the net, you're not jogging back down the floor. That basket ignites our defense and you're attacking someone in your assigned area immediately! I mean tough, hard-nose passing lane pressure defense. I want the guy throwing the ball in to be unsure about every inbounds pass. You

The Pressing Champions

have to tell yourself that you're not going to let the first receiver in your area get the ball.

"Look, there's a whole lot more to this pressing defense that we'll work on later, but this is our first objective. Anytime you cause the opponent to call timeout because of your defense, I look at that as a major victory because they just wasted a timeout that we forced them to take. Guess what? Your effort would've just earned us a free timeout, courtesy of our opponent.

From a coaching perspective, this should be a time of total positive reinforcement in the huddle because it came about as a direct result of our pressure defense. This would be the ideal time to let your team know that all that hard work in practice is now paying off.

So, now we could use that timeout to change the press, set up a play offensively, make substitutions. Hey, we could do a lot of things with that. I hate to waste timeouts because sometimes you need several of them late in the game, but I do love free timeouts.

"Roy, can you think of anything more deflating than not being able to get the ball in?"

Roy looked at me and with a sly smile said, "I see your point, Coach, and I can't think of anything worse than that."

Haywood gave me an intense look. "Coach, to me, this looks like it's perfect for our team. I can't wait, let's get it on!"

Coach Johnny Carter

Nubbin gave me a big smile and chipped in, "Looks like you designed this especially for me! I think I'm going to love this pressing defense."

Even though there was much more to the press than we discussed today, I loved the initial positive responses from my players.

As I left the gym, I wondered if they would have that same positive feeling once I implemented the intense conditioning workouts coming up.

With summer vacation fast approaching, it was Graduation Day and two of our players, Fred Pilkington and Danny Smith, were graduating. I was told by a former coach that graduation day was always bittersweet for him.

"You're always glad to see your players receive their diploma and move on with their lives, but you also realize that they've just finished their high school basketball career."

Fred would continue his basketball career as he'd received a scholarship to East Texas Baptist University. He would be sorely missed as he was a key player on our team.

After congratulating Danny and Fred, wishing them well, Herman approached me. "Mom invited you over for supper, if you don't have any plans."

"I don't have any plans, but if I did, I'd change them to have one of your mom's great meals."

The Pressing Champions

A meal with the Myers' family was indeed special. Mrs. Myers had invited me over numerous times and for that I would forever be grateful. Sitting around the table with Herman and his parents was Jeff and Nelda, his brother and sister. Jeff was in the eighth grade and the point guard on our talented junior high team. He had a lot of potential.

Nelda had definitely caught my eye as she was a stunningly beautiful brunette and also one of our cheerleaders. Oh, and by the way, she also had a lot of potential and I'm not talking about basketball. Too bad this gorgeous young girl was just a sophomore.

"Another delicious meal, Mrs. Myers. Thank you for inviting me."

"It's our pleasure having you here. Thanks for coming…and thank you for being our coach. What a special year!"

Mr. Myers said, "You did one heckuva job this year, Coach. Congratulations again!"

"Thank you, but in reality, the players got this done, I was just along for the ride."

Herman spoke up, "Coach, I know you're not one to pat yourself on the back, but the bottom line here is that you pushed us, you motivated us, you made us believe that we can go a lot farther than we ever thought we could. You know something else, every one of us loved playing for you."

Coach Johnny Carter

"Thank you, Herman, the feeling is mutual because I loved coaching you guys."

Nelda looked at me and said, "Speaking of love, I think every one of our cheerleaders has a crush on you."

I blushed and without thinking asked, "Does that include you?"

Totally catching her off guard, Nelda blushed. "Like I said, all of our cheerleaders."

I drove home with a big smile on my face that night.

Most of our players had summer jobs and I also had one. I enrolled at Sam Houston State University to continue work on my Master's degree. Working on my Master's was not the only reason I was going to be at Sam Houston. Archie Porter was the basketball coach and had previously won a state championship at Dallas's Thomas Jefferson High School using the full-court press. I planned to pick his brain as much as I could about his philosophy and implementation of the press. Coach Porter would be receptive to giving me some excellent ideas to use in teaching the press.

The summer vacation had barely gotten underway when one night I got a phone call from Herman.

"Coach, have you heard the news about Mr. Bitner?"

My heart skipped a beat. "Has something bad happened? Is he okay?"

"He's okay, Coach, that's the good news. The bad news is he's leaving."

The Pressing Champions

"What? Leaving, I can't believe it! Man, I like him. He took a chance and gave me a head-coaching job right out of college. I owe him a lot."

"I like him too, Coach. It won't be the same around here without him. He's been our superintendent for a long time."

"I'd heard some rumblings that there were some people dissatisfied, but I thought after we won the state championship, that might blow over. Apparently not!"

I was shocked. He'd been like a second father to me in my first year of coaching and I felt like I'd be lost without his guidance. This abrupt change in our school was a bad news/good news situation. The bad news was Mr. Bittner was gone and the good news was that our new superintendent, Clovis Van Deaver's wife, would assume the role as our new girls' coach, taking some of the load off of me.

The vacation passed quickly. as all summers seem to do. It was late August. Fall was fast approaching and my second year at Kennard was about to start.

After researching and talking to as many people as I could about the full-court press, I couldn't wait to start practice. My excited feeling about employing the press went right through the roof when I met one of our new players. Butch Walker was an absolutely perfect full-court press candidate. He had cat-like quickness and could run the floor like a deer. After a few days of practice, I was about to come to the conclusion that he could very well be one of our starting five. I knew what to expect out of my four returning seniors, but Butch, though unproven, had a ton of potential. So just what does potential mean? Well, basically it means you haven't done anything yet. Only time could tell.

Chapter 4
Never Enough Practice

Today's practice was underway and I was going through our numbering system on the position of each player with our press. In my mind, the ideal set up would be to have your most athletic post man as the guy on the ball.

That would be position number one. Numbers two and three would be your two wing men guarding the first man in their area with passing lane defense. Preferably, number four would be your point guard and the interceptor in the midcourt area. Ideally, your number five player would be your least athletic post man and the last line of defense. Although not etched in stone, this would be the preferred numbering scenario.

Today's emphasis was on the two and three positions which would contest the first inbounds pass. Seeing something that bothered me, I blew the whistle. I had a rule that when I blew the whistle, everybody froze in place. Noticing that a couple of guys didn't comply with this rule, I forcefully blew the whistle again and in a loud voice I said, "STOP! YOU KNOW THE RULE! WHEN I BLOW THIS WHISTLE, YOU DON'T TALK, YOU DON'T WALK, YOU DON'T EVEN BREATHE! YOU STOP, LOOK, AND LISTEN! IF YOU'RE IN THE AIR WHEN THE WHISTLE BLOWS, DON'T COME DOWN!"

With a sheepish grin on his face, Roy looked at me and said, "Come on, Coach. You know that's impossible."

With a raised eyebrow, I replied, "Do you get the point, Roy?"

Before he could answer, I added, "Do all of you get the point? Because if you don't, I'll be on your butt every day until you do, so you might as well learn that now! Is that clear, sports fans?"

There was a faint "yes sir" in the background.

"I can't hear you!"

Immediately, there was a much louder reply.

"Now that I have your complete attention, let's talk about the two and three spots on our pressing defense.

"First of all, you have to be extremely intense. I want every inbounds pass receiver to think that a swarm of bees is after him.

"Second, you have to position your body facing your man. Your arm nearest the ball is in the passing lane and using peripheral vision, your eyes can see both the ball and your man.

"Third, you do not let your man break between you and the ball. Each of you knows your own speed level, so adjust to what I'm saying here accordingly. If the guy you're guarding is much faster than you are, then cheat toward the ball to give yourself a chance to get the job done. If you're much quicker than the guy you're guarding, then you should be up his nose with your defense. I mean be on him like a leech. Obviously, this is not going to work every time because teams will get the ball in. When this happens, we're still pressing. We're just a little more conservative because getting back down the floor in a hurry can't be overstated. Giving up uncontested, easy baskets will not be tolerated!"

We accomplished a lot in today's practice and the concept of what I was trying to get across seemed to be sinking in. I was trying to make the fundamentals of our defense as simple as possible with major emphasis on effort and determination. If those two words describe your team, you're going to win a lot of games.

As I walked down the hall, the bell for third-period was about to ring for a change in classes. This wasn't the only change in our school. There was a huge change in women's fashion. Skirts were getting much shorter and the mini-skirt craze was just over the horizon.

Herman and Nubbin showed their approval as they walked to class. A beautiful young girl in a very short skirt definitely got their attention as she walked by them. Observing their reaction, I said, "Don't stare, you're making it too obvious. You've got to be a bit discreet!"

Herman looked at Nubbin with a big smile and then back at me.

"Coach, they wear those short skirts so we'll notice them. Besides, I know you like those short skirts as much as we do!"

"I can't disagree with that!" I said with a smile.

Nubbin and Herman were both laughing as they headed for their next class.

Coach Johnny Carter

What I didn't tell them was that those short skirts did indeed make it difficult for a young, single, male teacher to concentrate in class. After all, I was human and only a few years older than the students.

Our practices were getting more intense as the change in our style of play came into effect. One thing that we hadn't changed was that we still were using the same weight vest workout that we used last year. It was both psychologically and physically good for our team and I saw no reason to change that.

On the other hand, I was constantly trying to come up with different drills that could capture game-like situations. I had begun using the 11-break drill, a continuous full court three-on-two drill that I had designed last year; however, something was missing in this drill that kept it from being exactly what we needed.

One day, I got the idea of adding full-court press principles to the drill. This was the exact change that it needed for us to get the game-like simulation that I was looking for. What I liked the most about this change was that it created a conditioned response for igniting inbounds pass pressure. This was such an important part of the basic press philosophy that I wanted to employ.

The advantage of this drill was that the players did not look at it as a conditioning drill because they had a lot of fun running it. Basically, the 11-break drill was disguised conditioning and that is the best kind by far.

The Pressing Champions

This was a welcome change from just lining guys up and running sprints at the end of practice.

Most coaches look at running sprints as a necessary evil. Players view this as a boring part of the game and usually don't run as hard as they do when filling the lane on a fast break. The 11-break drill was great for the fast break and with the addition of the full-court press principles, it became a perfect drill for our team.

Adding a few free-throw breaks made it as close to a true game-like simulation as I could find. It would become a regular part of our daily practice and the players absolutely loved it.

Practice should be a learning experience. When your players have fun with its implementation, this is when you get so much more accomplished. This drill would become a major part of our daily practice the rest of my coaching career.

I was sitting in the cafeteria, talking with Benford Frizzell, our Ag teacher. As I took a sip of coffee, he looked at me, he asked, "Well, how is practice going?"

"It's going well. I'm totally sold on the pressing defense."

About that time, Curtis Baker came into the cafeteria and joined us.

Benford looked at me. "Coach, I have to ask this question. Some of our fans are very concerned about the big changes you've made."

Curtis nodded his head and said, "I'm hearing some of the same things, Coach."

"Listen, fellas, I know more about my team than any of the guys talking to you. I'm 100% positive about the pressing defense. It teaches intensity, determination, all-out hustle, and I can't leave out the fact that there's always the potential to turn a game around in a short period of time. Look, this type of game fits me like a glove. I think it's absolutely perfect for our team. In fact, I wish we'd used this when I played in high school. I think we might have won the state championship had we pressed."

Curtis looked me in the eye and said, "That's good enough for me, Coach. I've been sold on you for a long time."

Benford laughed. "I didn't want to bring this up because I thought it might worry you, but I can see that it doesn't. If you're that positive about what you're doing, go for it!"

Hearing part of the conversation while pouring me some fresh coffee, Nona said, "Coach, whatever you do, don't let some fan tell you how to coach your team. Fans are just fans. They probably mean well, but they have no idea what goes on in that gym every day."

I must admit that I was a little bit concerned about what I was hearing, but I wasn't about to change anything that I was doing.

Benford looked at me. "Coach, you got a minute? I've got something I want to show you."

The Pressing Champions

We walked down the hall into the gym.

With a look of accomplishment on his face, Benford gestured toward the wall behind our bench. "Well, how do you like it?"

To my astonishment, his vocational agriculture shop class had constructed an exact replica of the huge state map as seen in the background at the state tournament.

"Man, that is beautiful! You've even got the colored lights geographically locating every state tournament participant. I love it! That's definitely going to help intimidate our opponents. Thank you."

Chapter 5
A New Look

My short drive to school from Crockett had extra meaning as I listened to Paul Harvey's news and commentary. Our pre-season workouts were over and we were about to play our first game of the season.

It was hard to believe that it had been a year to the day when I coached the first game of my life. With the big changes that I'd made in our style of play, I was anxious to see the result of all our long hours of hard work.

Butch Walker emerged as our fifth starter. He was slowly adjusting to a new environment and a different style of play. Overall, our team seemed to be grasping the basics and fundamentals of what I was trying to teach. They definitely seemed to like this new style of play.

As I walked from my car into the school building, I saw Roy and Haywood standing in the hallway talking.

When he saw me, Roy turned and said, "Good morning, Coach. Do you think we're ready for tonight?"

"I think so, what do you guys think?"

Always with a positive smile, Haywood replied, "You know I'm always ready and I think that this press is going to give our opponents a whole lot of problems."

"I think you're right. Hey, before you guys go to class, come down to the dressing room, I want to show you something."

The Pressing Champions

Opening a box, I pulled out a brand-new uniform that we'd be wearing tonight. "How do you guys like these?"

Haywood looked at Roy. They were both smiling.

Haywood said, "Coach, I can do some damage wearing these."

I then showed them our new purple knee socks with a white 'K' on the side.

Roy smiled again. "Coach, we're gonna be lookin' good tonight."

I grinned. "When you look good, you better play good!"

"Don't worry, Coach, we're going to do that."

As I walked to class, I had a smile on my face and my heart felt easy.

Illustration by my son, John Carter

Chapter 6
The Second Season

Benford was driving the bus as we were getting close to New Summerfield, the plant capitol of the south. With several greenhouses on both sides of the road, this nursery-driven community was just over the horizon.

Though a little bit nervous about our first game, I was not nearly as nervous as I was a year ago on this date. The big advantage would be that I would not be coaching the girls' game, but concentrating totally on the upcoming boys' contest.

With my team sitting before me, dressed out and ready to go, I was going over some reminders for our first game of the season.

"You guys are more than ready for this game. Just remember what we've worked on with the press. Butch,

The Pressing Champions

you've got the number five spot. Tell me what you're supposed to do with that."

"I'm the back guy, the last line of defense. If they get through the press, my job is to slow them down and defend the basket."

"Remember, Butch, you never go for a steal unless you're 100% sure that you can get the ball. If you miss, they're going to score and it will be your fault. If there's any doubt in your mind, then fake going for the steal and go back and guard the basket. Is that clear, son?"

"Yes sir, I've got it, Coach."

"Herman, you've got the number four spot. Tell me what your main job is."

"I take the third receiver and cheat toward the ball. If somebody snowbirds and takes off early, I then become the number five guy momentarily."

"Herman, you know that you have the toughest job on the floor, defending the inbounds pass because you have to wait and see who the third man is.

"Roy, you and Nubbin are taking the two and three spots. I expect you to eat the two guys in your area alive. Try your best to force your man to the sideline because that's double-team territory. We want to contest the diagonal pass from the trap to the middle of the floor.

"Don't worry about the horizontal pass along the baseline because that pass does not move the ball up the floor. We'll give them that pass and when that happens, we're basically going back to man defense and not double teaming at that moment.

"Haywood, you're the number one guy—the intimidator. Once the ball is passed to the corner, you're over there in a flash, double-teaming. Remember the rotation that we worked on and execute it quickly!

"Any questions? Okay everyone. take a knee, let's have our prayer."

We started the game on a high note as the press really caught New Summerfield off-balance. They weren't ready for our aggressive inbounds pass pressure as it created a bunch of turnovers, resulting in several easy baskets.

Roy and Nubbin had a field day creating many steals and turnovers. All of the hard work in practice paid off and I was thrilled with our execution, effort, and determination.

We made our share of easily correctable mistakes, but we had total hustle, resulting in a convincing 79-39 opening game victory. In fact, our press continued to improve as we decisively won our next three games in the same manner as the first one.

With each practice and game, we were becoming more positive about pressure defense. When you experience success after many long hours of practice, it reconfirms what that hard work is all about. This creates a mindset of positivity that hopefully will carry us through the entire season.

It was early morning and I was sitting in the cafeteria with Curtis, discussing our next opponent,

The Pressing Champions

Woden. Curtis had scouted several teams for me last year and was giving me a report on the Eagles.

"Coach, I believe they're better than they were last year. You and I both know how impressed we were with them at the regional tournament."

"That doesn't surprise me, Curtis, because we both know that they're extremely well-coached. Keith Lowry does a great job with those guys, so we have our work cut out for us when we go over there tomorrow night."

"One more thing, Coach, I think we're going to be a whole lot better this year. That full-court press looks better every time we play. Man, I love what you're doing with this team."

"Thanks, Curtis, I really appreciate that. The Woden game will be our first true test and we'll see just how this new approach works against a real good team."

"Good luck, Coach."

That day in practice, I was working on the rotation after the trap on the press.

"Okay, Haywood and Nubbin set the trap up in the corner. Roy, you're going to rotate here quickly to cut off the diagonal pass to the middle.

"Herman, you bust it here to cut off that up-the-floor sideline pass. Fellas, when you cut off those two passes, you're encouraging the cross court, meaningless baseline pass which does not move the ball up the floor. If they do make that pass, we quickly rotate again into a straight man defense. We don't want to trap when the ball is in the middle of the floor."

So, basically, we changed our defense three times on their two passes.

"Listen, Roy, you do have the option to go for the steal on that baseline pass. So, what happens if you don't get the steal?"

"I'll get the steal, Coach!"

"I like your positive attitude, but there'll be times when you don't and when that happens, I'd better see you other four guys on your racehorse getting back into the paint!

"Roy, when that happens, I want to see you plant your foot, come out of the starting blocks like Bob Hayes and get back down the floor in a hurry!

"Okay, let's practice this and see how quickly we can rotate to these spots."

We worked on this rotation over and over because I wanted it to be an automatic reaction.

Curtis was right on with his scouting report. Woden was indeed spot on and they were well-prepared for this game. Having a ton of incentive to knock off the defending state champion, they gave us all we wanted and then some. I also realized that we'd be facing teams all year with this extra incentive to beat us and that was something we'd have to deal with. The game was nip-and-tuck well into the fourth quarter. Late in the game, with Woden leading by two, Butch Walker left his

The Pressing Champions

number five spot, going all out for a steal and leaving the basket unattended. This resulted in an easy basket and Woden went on to a 61-55 win.

In the dressing room after the game, I looked at Butch and said, "I'm not blaming you for this loss. There are lots of things we could've done differently to change the outcome; however, you didn't do what I told you to do."

With sadness in his eyes, he looked at me and said, "Coach, I thought I could get the ball."

"I don't want you to THINK you can get the ball...I WANT YOU KNOW YOU CAN GET THE BALL! Is that clear? There's never a good time to make a mistake, but since you made one, let that be a lesson learned. Better now than later. Albert Einstein once said, 'A person who never made a mistake never tried anything new.' Look, Butch, I'm glad you tried to get that steal. The effort was there, but the end result was not. This is an easy, correctable mistake. My job as your coach is to teach you exactly how I want that situation handled."

With a serious look on my face, I looked at Butch and said, "Look, son, you're an excellent player and I have a ton of confidence in you. You're going to help us win a lot of games this year; just don't ever let that happen again!"

I reached out, shook his hand and said, "Deal?"

"Yes sir."

One thing I always tried to do when correcting a player was to let the correction be a part and sometimes a small part of an uplifting compliment. That way you make the positive override the negative, but you still get the point across in a manner that does not put a player down. You never want to destroy a player's confidence and some guys are extremely sensitive. For this reason, it's imperative that you know each player's personality because everybody is different. Some guys only need a pat on the back while others need a kick in the butt in order for them to perform to the utmost of their ability. Some players can be very challenging and for that reason a coach needs to figure out what makes each player tick and coach them accordingly. I am a firm believer that you can't coach everybody the same way.

As I paced in front of my team, I stopped in my tracks and said, "Look, we forced plenty of turnovers – enough to win this game; however, we only shot 28%! Hey, there will be other games when we don't shoot well and this takes away full-court press opportunities. I have an idea about a change we can make with our press that will help this. Surprisingly, even though we shot poorly, we almost won this game anyway. Why? One reason: THE PRESS! It kept us in the game! Without it, we would've been killed tonight. Besides, we do play them at home later this season. Remember this night. Remember this when they come to our house!

"And one more thing...I know you know this already, but win or lose, I will always love you guys. Now, let's get on the bus and go home."

The Pressing Champions

Learning how to accept a loss was something that I had to really work at. With only four losses all last year, basically, I was spoiled. There's a silver lining to a loss and that is practice the next day.

As I walked into the gym, I couldn't wait to start today's practice. Good teams and good players always seem to be a little more receptive to coaching after a loss. They want to do whatever they can to make sure it doesn't happen again. This was obviously the case today as our players were totally focused on improving our game.

Nearing the end of practice, we had already reviewed several of the correctable errors made last night. I always seemed to be stressing the importance of a strong defense and today was no exception. I was in the process of emphasizing our half-court man-to-man. Our starting five were going against Gary Parrish, Walter Denman, Richard Curry, Eddie Ray Pilkington, and Leeland Strban.

Seeing something that disturbed me, I immediately blew my whistle.

"Stop! Freeze! Stay right where you are! Herman, do you think you're where you should be?"

"I think so."

"Look where the ball is. It's on the other side of the floor from you. You're playing Gary like he has the ball. Have you ever seen a guy make a shot that did not have the ball?"

With a sheepish smile, Herman replied, "It's not possible."

"Look, my point is this." Moving toward the ball and with one foot in the paint, I said, "Herman, I'm going to play your spot for a second. Gary, when you get the ball, I want you to take a shot. Walter, I want you to pass the ball cross-court all the way over to Gary."

As he did, I quickly rushed out to Gary, getting in correct defensive position with a hand in his face. Gary didn't have a wide-open shot.

Walking back toward the basket, I looked at Herman and said, "So, why are you out there holding hands with Gary when you can do the same job here? How many times in practice have you heard me say 'cheat toward the ball'?"

"A lot."

"Guess what? you're going to hear this a lot the rest of this year, whether I'm talking about our half-court or full-court defense. Doing this is what I call 'helping defense' and it's one of the keys for it being successful. Like everything else about this sport, defense has a team objective, but if one person doesn't do their job individually, it weakens the productivity."

Looking at the rest of the team, I said, "Defense is all about where the ball is. You always have to know where the ball is because it determines where you should be and what you should do. If the ball moves and you don't, guess where you're going to be?" I pointed toward our bench. "Sitting right beside me over there."

The Pressing Champions

"Okay, let's try this again and see if we can do it the right way." Showing a newly defined emphasis on proper half-court defensive principles, at least for today, we appeared to be on the right track.

November was just around the corner as fall was about to evolve into winter. The seasonal change had the leaves starting to trickle down from the treetops. An early morning rain not only cooled the atmosphere, but released even more leaves that slowly drifted down, fluttering in the breeze. We were well into second period as I walked down the hall toward the cafeteria to have another cup of coffee and read the paper.

Before entering the cafeteria, I looked down the hall and saw Nelda Myers headed toward me. She walked right up to me and said, "Sorry about the loss to Woden!"

I looked at this beautiful young girl and said, "We played well enough to win, but when you shoot a very poor percentage, most of the time you come out second. We did come out first in one category, though."

Not understanding what I was talking about, she gave me an inquisitive look and asked, "Just what category did we win last night?"

With a slight grin, I said, "The cheerleader contest. With you out there leading our cheerleaders, we definitely finished first!"

Nelda blushed, then smiled. "Thanks, Coach, I really appreciate that. I didn't know you even noticed."

"Believe me, I noticed!" I assured her.

Coach Johnny Carter

She smiled and then headed down the hall with a look of surprise and satisfaction on her face.

That loss motivated our team in a much bigger way than I ever dreamed it would. The intensity level on our full-court press, which was already pretty good, got much better. Our inbounds pass pressure began to pay dividends as it really rattled a lot of teams. We were learning the ins-and-outs of this new style of play and adapting well to its execution.

Learning how to apply hard-nose pressure without fouling was something that we worked on every day. It took a lot of repetitious practice for this to reach the level I wanted. Today, we were adding a new phase to our pressing defense that I'd been thinking about incorporating for quite some time. After the Woden game, I was convinced that it needed to be done.

Basically, this was a 2-2-1 half-court press. Our regular full-court press was triggered exclusively by a made basket. So, in other words, we had to score to use it. My main concern was what would happen if we had a poor shooting game and that's exactly what happened in our only loss of the year. The end result was we ran the full-court press much less than normal.

My new idea would be to use the 2-2-1 when we did not score and our full-court press when we did. This could be accomplished because a player could set up the 2-2-1 as he retreated to the other end. It was another big change in what we were doing and I planned on gradually incorporating this into our game plan.

In explaining this I said, "This is going to make our overall defense much better because it adds another way for us to apply pressure."

Looking at Butch, I added, "This is going to be a big change in what your assignment is at the number five position because with this you're going to gamble and try to steal every pass down the sideline. It's just the opposite of what you do on the full-court press.

"Listen, any of you running the number five spot on our 2-2-1, you've got to know what you're doing. We'll practice this a lot before it becomes part of our game plan. I want you to know this backwards and forwards."

We had reeled off seven consecutive, mostly lopsided victories leading up to the Madisonville tournament. This tournament was one of the oldest continuously operating tournaments in the state and once again was loaded with good teams. It was just a year ago that our team took off to a long winning streak after Snook defeated us in the semi-finals. Hoping to continue our current winning streak, we soundly defeated Buffalo and Hearne in early round games and got by Huntsville in the semi-finals.

On the other side of the bracket, Snook also reached the finals. So, the earlier cancellation by Snook was about to be played anyway as two former state champions would collide in the finals.

Coach Johnny Carter

Although it was not as big of a deal as it was last year, we once again spent the night in my parents' home. Mom and Dad loved having my team in their home and this was one of the major reasons for the success of our team a year ago. It solidified the ever-developing required togetherness that a team needs if it's going to become special. Hopefully this would give us that little something extra that it would take for us to be successful in our big game tonight.

I was totally blessed to have grown up in this house with two extra-special, very loving parents and two great brothers. I wish every kid had a mom and dad like mine. Their positive influence and direction in my life cannot be overstated.

We were enjoying an incredible country style lunch of Mom's special meatloaf, mashed potatoes, turnip greens, cornbread, and her delicious cucumber salad.

"Wow, Mom! This is so tasty! Thank you!"

Herman looked up from his meal and said, "Mrs. Carter, this is a great meal. Just make sure that Lester over there gets a couple of helpings. We need to put some more meat on his bones."

With a big smile, Lester looked up from his plate and said, "Just make sure that Herman just has one plate because he needs to lose a couple of pounds."

Mom smiled. She absolutely loved preparing this great meal for my team and our players felt quite at home here.

The Pressing Champions

After the meal, I told my guys to make themselves at home, lounge around, stay off their feet, and get as much rest as they could because we would soon be playing our second game of the day.

Fortunately, I was able to take our starters out early against Huntsville, giving them a little extra rest because we were in command, winning by 23.

Dad had been unusually quiet during our meal. Before he left to go back to work, he called me outside.

"Well, son, what's your thought about tonight's game?"

"I'm sure they'll keep the score low and if they get a lead, they'll go to their famous delay game. You and I both know that they're highly disciplined and run that clock-killing delay tactic with precision."

Dad smiled. "Just don't get behind!"

With a serious look on my face, I looked at Dad and said, "That's exactly what we're going to try to do, but that's easier said than done. If we're going to win this game, we're going to have to play much better than we've been playing and we are definitely capable of doing that. I really don't think that we've come close to reaching our peak. Hopefully, tonight we'll take a giant step in that direction. I think we're ready and our guys are looking forward to this game."

"Good luck, son."

Later that afternoon, I was talking with Herman.

"Let's go for a walk, son, I'd like to visit with you about this game."

Coach Johnny Carter

As we walked down the street adjacent to our house, I looked at my highly proficient point guard and said, "Up to now, this will be our biggest game of the year. Look, Snook is hard to beat. Their style of play pretty much dictates that. They play great defense and make very few mistakes.

"I've talked to you before about my senior year and losing in the regional finals to Buna. They were coached by Cotton Robinson, winner of seven state championships and probably the most successful high school coach in Texas basketball history. Jimmy Horn, Snook's coach, is a product of Buna basketball and much of what he does is influenced by Cotton Robinson. I think this is one of the main reasons why they've been so successful. You know when they got that lead on us last year and went into their delay game, it was pretty much over. We can't let that affect our game if they do get a lead.

"Son, I'm counting on you to do everything you can to keep our mindset positive out there on that floor. I know you've pretty much been doing that, but tonight in particular, I want to re-emphasize just how important that is. I think many times Snook just flat out totally frustrates teams into a loss. We can't let that happen tonight. I'm counting on you to make sure that we implement our game plan, regardless of what they do."

"You can count on me, Coach. We're not going to let those guys beat us again! Last year was last year. We're

The Pressing Champions

a totally different team this year and with our pressing defense, we're a much better team."

Chapter 7

Snook

Snook, Texas is located some fourteen miles west of Bryan/College Station, near the Brazos River. It was settled by Czech farmers who took advantage of the rich, fertile, river bottom land.

In 1895, the community attempted to obtain a post office. John S. Snook, the postmaster of nearby Caldwell, Texas, arranged for the post office to be established. The new post office was named "Snook" in his honor and later became the name of the town.

Looking into the faces of my team prior to the finals of the Madisonville tournament, I said, "I am highly disgusted that Snook called and canceled the two games that we had scheduled with them for this year.

"Most of you remember when we played them in the semi-finals of this tournament last year. At that time, they were the two-time defending state champions. That particular game was a turning point for our team because it not only woke us up, but it let us know that we were good enough to play with the best.

"We took off like a rocket after that loss and we came together as a team in a huge way. Prior to that game, we'd played pretty well, but after that game, we stepped up to

The Pressing Champions

a much higher level and really were a totally different team the rest of the season.

"Hey, that was last year and what we do out there on that floor right now…well, this is this year and a whole new season. Look at me, fellas. It's payback time! We owe these guys one! When we played them last year, they were on their way to a 90-game winning streak. Every game they played they were facing a team with extra motivation to knock off a state champion. Well, guess what? That situation is reversed and now they're trying to do the same thing that we tried to do last year. I look at this as a state championship game and if we do face these guys again, it'll be in Austin at the state tournament. I'm telling you right now, you're a better team than they are, but there's one catch—you've got to go out there and prove it. You know if they get a lead that they're going to try to put the game in the icebox. They're highly disciplined and make very few mistakes, so if they do get a lead, be patient defensively. They'll try to lull you to sleep, attempting to get an easy basket."

With a stern look on my face, I asked, "DO YOU WANT TO WIN THIS GAME?" There was a very positive response from everyone in the room.

Roy looked at me and asked, "What do we have to do to win this game?"

I smiled and said, "It's all about how hard we play on defense. This has been our strength all year long. Right now, we need to step it up to a different level. Can we do this?"

Coach Johnny Carter

Nubbin looked at me and said, "We can and we will, right guys?" Again, there was another emotionally charged response.

Looking at my very amped-up team, I said, "Keep your head in the game and whatever you do, DO NOT LET UP ON DEFENSE! Is that clear, sports fans?"

There was a very positive response. It certainly seemed that my message had gotten through.

"There's a massive crowd out there awaiting this game. Let's go out there and put on a show. Give all those fans, as well as the Blue Jays, a taste of Tiger basketball."

The strategy that Snook used was exactly what I expected. They tried to keep the score low and did. It was to our advantage having played them last year because we adapted to their game and met the challenge. Unlike last year, we didn't let their strategy alter what we did. Our full-court pressure, as well as our half-court defense, paid some big-time dividends and we managed to win 35 to 31.

It was particularly gratifying for our players and our fans, some of whom didn't think we'd win this game.

My dad came up to me after the game and gave me a big hug, offering his congratulations. I could tell by the look in his eyes that he was overjoyed with what had just transpired.

"I'm so proud of you, son! This was a great win, but you know I'd still be proud of you even if you'd lost."

The Pressing Champions

Before going to the dressing room, I gave Mom and Dad a hug. With a look of love, I simply said, "Thank you."

Our dressing room was electric! Haywood gripped my hand with a vicious handshake "That's what I'm talking about, Coach!"

Nubbin had a smile on his face when he came up to me and shook my hand. "How 'bout that defense, Coach? You said we needed to play great defense tonight to win this game and that's exactly what we did! We're improving, Coach. We're getting better every game."

"You've got that right, son."

By winning our 11th straight game, our confidence level went right through the roof. In analyzing the tournament after all was said and done, it was particularly fulfilling that three of the teams that we soundly defeated enroute to the championship advanced to the final round and took home a trophy.

Walking down the hall this chilly Monday morning in December, I had a little extra bounce in my step, looking forward to a cup of coffee. The first sip tasted extra special.

I walked over to the window and looked outside. It was a typical, dreary, overcast winter morning in East Texas. The north wind was whipping through the pines and the temperature was getting close to freezing.

The cafeteria door swung open and Curtis walked in with a smile on his face. Rubbing his hands together, he said, "Brrrr...it's getting cold out there! Good morning, Coach! Now tell me the truth, how does it feel to beat the Blue Jays?"

I looked at Curtis. "Can't you tell? Last year after we played those guys, our team blossomed."

"Any prediction this year?"

"No prediction, Curtis, but I will say this, we're definitely getting better. I see it in practice every day and now it's carrying over to our games. I guess we'll find out what effect this big win has on our team tomorrow night when we have our rematch game against Woden."

"Well, since you're not going to make a prediction, I'm going to make one. I think we're going to kick Woden's butt tomorrow night."

I smiled as I headed to my first period class. The huge win over Snook couldn't have come at a better time because it fueled the fire for our second game with Woden. This was the team responsible for the only blemish on our schedule. Our little gym was jam-packed, standing-room-only. Fans were sitting on the floor along the baseline and the sidelines. People were standing behind all the occupied chairs on the stage. Several late arriving fans had no place to sit or stand and were turned away because the exits were jammed.

Looking at my fired-up team in the huddle, I said, "Remember what they did to you guys at their place? Well, now they're at our house and it's time to return the favor. If you can't play your hardest with a crowd like that out there, then it can't be done! Let's show these guys who the real boss is!"

With our highly partisan crowd constantly roaring in the background and the revenge factor providing a ton of extra incentive, we were more than ready, took control early, and using a relentless, ferocious full-court press forced numerous turnovers and won going away 72-50.

I was always stressing team balance and this game proved to be just that. Roy Harrison led all scorers with 22 points. Haywood had 17, Herman 15, and Butch got 10. After a slow start at the beginning of the season, Butch was now blending in nicely with our four returning starters. Our defense was superb, holding their best player, Charles Woodson, to a team high of only 10 points.

Before I could get to the dressing room, my dad rushed up to me with a pleased smile on his face and gave me a hug.

"Son, you have really got this team playing hard. That full-court press is something else! We totally dominated a very good team out there tonight."

About that time, Miss Nona came up and gave me a big hug. "Congratulations, Coach! This team just gets better every time I watch them play. Our fans are starting to really love this new style of play. It's so exciting!"

With a smirk on my face, I looked at her and said, "That oughta be worth another fried pie!"

"It's worth a lot more than that, Coach!"

Coach Johnny Carter

With that said, I headed for the dressing room.

For the second straight game, our already high level of confidence was mushrooming. Our dressing room now resembled a churning sea of excitement. Smiles, laughter, high-fives, and pats on the back were all part of the congratulatory gestures in evidence.

I was met at the door by Herman who had a radiant look on his face and his patented smile.

"Congratulations, Coach! That's the best we've played all year. We can't play much better than that."

"Come on, Herman, what have I taught you guys? You know we can always get better."

He gave me a serious look. "I have to admit that I had doubts at the beginning about full-court pressure defense, but you were right all along. It's absolutely perfect for our team and boy does it give other teams the blues. We should've used that last year."

I looked at him out of the corner of my eye and said, "Yeah, who knows, we just might've won the state championship!"

Now Herman and I were both laughing, as was everybody else in this joyful dressing room.

Herman gave me a mischievous look and said, "Coach, you've always said that you love us win or lose. Do you love us more when we win?"

I laughed "Get your butt out of here."

The Pressing Champions

After winning our last two games against two highly competitive teams, my first cup of coffee tasted absolutely great. Benford and Curtis were sitting across the table discussing last night. Never at a loss for words, Benford looked at me and with the insight of a Mark Twain-like statement, he said, "Funny thing, Coach. All those guys who doubted the change you made in the style of play, well guess what they are now?" He hesitated one second before adding, "Your biggest fans!"

We were all laughing "It's funny what winning can do," said Curtis. "It can make someone go from left to right in a second!"

With a strong wind at our back, raising our confidence level to an all-time high, our winning streak spiraled to fifteen when we convincingly defeated Tomball 88 to 70. That weekend we traveled the short distance to Crockett to play in their tournament, attempting to repeat as last year's champion.

The town of Crockett has a very interesting history. It was named after Davy Crockett, who camped near the townsite on his way to the Alamo in January 1836. Houston County was established a year later, shortly after General Sam Houston's makeshift Texas volunteers surprised and defeated a much larger Mexican army in the battle of San Jacinto. After gaining independence from Mexico, the county was named after Sam Houston, who would become the first president of the new republic of Texas.

Coach Johnny Carter

After winning the first two games, we met the host team in the finals in an all Houston County shootout before a standing-room-only crowd. Record numbers traveled from near and far to witness this game, which was the largest crowd ever to see a game in the Crockett gym.

Roy and Herman hit 20 and 18 points, respectively, to lead us to a 58 to 43 victory, while Sam Bruce, Crockett's best player, got 14 for the Bulldogs.

At the end of the game, Herman looked at me and made a serious comment. "It's a shame the rules wouldn't let Sam transfer because he definitely wanted to play with us."

"There's no doubt about it, he could definitely help us!"

As I walked off the floor, Curtis and Nona came up to me. Nona said, "Well, Coach, you just earned yourself a whole bunch of apricot fried pies."

"You mean to tell me that I have to beat Crockett to keep getting those tasty pies?"

She smiled as she exited the gym.

It was December and the temperature was getting much colder. All the deciduous trees that were so beautiful in the spring and fall now displayed a seasonal personality. With totally bare limbs, the large, majestic oak that I passed by on my way to school every morning now had a skeletal appearance. On the other hand, the tall slender pines that totally engulfed our landscape still had their gorgeous evergreen look, synonymous with Christmas.

In fact, it was the week before Christmas. I was sitting alone in the cafeteria early this Monday morning when Miss Nona emerged from the kitchen, refreshed my coffee, and handed me a warm apricot fried pie.

I grinned at her. "Since we did beat Crockett, does that mean I get fried pies the rest of the year?"

"Hey, no one, even Curtis is more pleased about beating Crockett than I am, but that might be stretching it a bit too far. You still have a lot of games left. In fact, you have two more this week."

We did have to play Big Sandy and Rusk before the Holidays. Riding the crest of a powerful wave of momentum, we won those two games going away, extending our winning streak to twenty consecutive games.

It was the last day of school before the Christmas break. The students were wired, anticipating the two-week vacation. Everyone looked forward to the Holidays to spend some time away from school and celebrate Christmas. There's usually not much teaching going on this last day. That was the case with my sixth period science class. When the bell sounded, I wished everyone a Merry Christmas and then headed to the gym.

At the end of the hallway, I saw Nelda coming toward me.

"Wait up, Coach, I have something for you. Miss Nona told me to bring this to you and to wish you a Merry Christmas."

With that she handed me a plate covered with aluminum foil.

"Is this what I think it is?"

Nelda smiled. "It is and she said to take these pies home and share them with your family for Christmas."

I looked at her and said, "Be sure to thank her for me and, by the way, when are you gonna make me a pie?"

Catching her off-guard, she looked back at me as she walked away. "You never know."

With as good a feeling as a young coach could have at the midpoint of the season, I headed home for the Holidays. The beauty of Christmas lights dotted both sides of the highway as I drove through Crockett enroute to Madisonville. I always enjoyed going home, but being home for Christmas was extra special.

Getting away from the grind of the season was going to be good for me and my players. However, when your team is 24-1 at the break, you're hoping that this pause in the schedule doesn't erode your momentum.

It was wonderful visiting with my parents and my two brothers during the Holidays. Too often what this time of the year is all about gets lost in the commercialism of the season. Fortunately, when we were kids, my mom and dad taught us the true meaning of Christmas; something we would never forget.

The Pressing Champions

In the Centerville tournament after the Holidays, we never missed a beat. Winning all three games without really being challenged, our team won this tournament for the second straight year. The district race was right around the corner and it appeared that we were more than ready for the challenge.

The one concern that bothered me most right now was that we had very few games that were close. You need a tight game every now and then so you know how to react to a pressure situation. Sooner or later, you'll have a game that really matters and you won't be ready for it. We had been so dominant most of the season that we really hadn't been tested. I never wanted to run an opponent into the ground and totally embarrass them, but by the same token, I wanted our main players to get enough playing time to merit having a game in the first place. Had I left my starters in the game, we would've averaged a lot more points per game, but in my opinion, this really would not have accomplished our goal.

Much to the dismay of my players, I took them out earlier than they wanted to come off the floor. This, in turn, gave me a chance to play some of our younger guys in varsity games, giving them invaluable experience for the future.

Three of our JV starters suited up with the varsity when they didn't have a game and I worked them into as many varsity games as possible. Lester Hutcherson and James Smith were sophomores. Jeff Myers was a freshman. These three guys, along with freshmen Donald Denman and Carl Watson, had the makings of a good team for the future. They played against our varsity daily, almost always coming out second; however, they were learning how to go against guys that were much better.

I've always thought that if you go against somebody that's more talented, you better work your tail off so you won't get embarrassed. This is what these guys were facing every day in practice. I could tell by their work ethic that down the road this was going to be beneficial. You never know when one of your players might foul out or get hurt and you have to go to your bench in a crucial situation.

We arrived home very late from the Centerville tournament and I was on my way to Madisonville to spend the rest of the weekend with my family. The clock said 12:00 a.m. as I crossed the Trinity River bridge. It was now New Year's Eve, December 31, 1967.

After a much-needed good night's rest, a Sunday church service, and another one of my mom's special home-cooked lunches, it was time for the NFL championship.

In a game that would later be called "The Ice Bowl" Dallas was playing in Green Bay, Wisconsin under absolutely the most terrible weather conditions imaginable. The temperature was a miserable -15°F with a wind chill of -48°F. The game featured two future Hall of Fame head coaches pitted against each other—Tom Landry of the Cowboys and Vince Lombardi of the

The Pressing Champions

Packers. Tom Landry was an inspiration to me. I admired him as both a man and a coach. Despite my dad and I pulling hard for the up-and-coming Cowboys, the Packers survived the cold, winning 21 to 17.

At the game's conclusion, my dad looked at me and said, "It's a shame that a game of that importance has to be played under those conditions."

Chapter 8

Cheat Toward the Ball

It was January and although not nearly as cold as it was in Green Bay, nonetheless it was the dead of winter in East Texas. A blistering blue norther had just arrived, considerably dropping the temperature. It was cold and the howling wind outside made it seem even colder.

Inside it was hot or I should say, I was hot! We were scrimmaging against our JV team and believe it or not, they were giving us all we wanted. Occasionally, they gave us more competition than some of the teams we played.

This indeed was a bittersweet scenario. On the one hand, you're glad that your young guys' potential is starting to develop because, after all, this was our team of the future. On the other hand, your varsity players are there because they're supposed to be better and should play accordingly. However, we definitely needed to be challenged and today we were. Seeing something that I didn't like, I forcefully blew my whistle.

"Okay, go back to where you were. James Smith, you had the ball and passed it to Lester. Haywood, you were guarding James and he went right between you and the ball! What are you supposed to do when the ball is passed?"

The Pressing Champions

Haywood had a frustrated look on his face. He looked at me and said, "Cheat to the ball, but Coach, James is fast!"

"Is he faster than you?"

"Probably."

"I know James is fast, but I also know there's no way he should go between you and the ball. He beat you because you didn't react. You know what you're supposed to do. You were *thinking* what you're supposed to do, I don't want that! I want you *doing* what you're supposed to do!

"Do the rest of you guys understand what I'm talking about? Roy, Herman, Butch, Nubbin – all the rest of you guys! Now, Haywood, show me you can play the kind of defense I've taught you."

Haywood then very competitively showed me that dominant defensive skill that I was looking for; in fact, the whole team did.

Leading up to our first district game, our defense showed remarkable improvement that very day. Again, this was brought about to a large extent by being challenged by our ever-improving JV team.

We were about to start what I call "the second season." These are the games that count and determine whether or not you're even in the playoffs. Curtis and I had scouted every team in the district and we felt really good about our chances.

Coach Johnny Carter

With one game remaining before the district schedule, we traveled the long distance south to Tomball, convincingly winning 67 to 35.

Later that week, the district race started with a rush as we raced by our first two opponents, Centerville (Groveton) and Lovelady, leading up to Apple Springs, the team with the best chance of defeating us. We had already convincingly defeated them in the first round of the Crockett tournament, but I was sure that they'd try something different the second time. That's exactly what they did as they tried to slow the pace down and keep the score low. To a degree, this was partially successful; however, we adjusted our game and won going away 52 to 36. With Herman, Roy, and Butch each scoring 13 points, while Haywood got 12, we put new meaning to the term "balanced scoring." With Nubbin leading our team with his consistent hawking defense, we held a pretty decent team to only 36 points. The Eagles were led in scoring by Paul Cook and Eugene Brooks, their two best players with 18 and 10 points, respectively.

In our last game of the first round, we had little trouble defeating Redland by 21 points.

The Pressing Champions

It was Saturday, January 20, 1968. I was on my way to Houston with my two brothers to watch the number one ranked undefeated UCLA Bruins go against my alma mater, the number two ranked undefeated University of Houston Cougars. The Astrodome was filled to capacity as 52,693 exuberant fans were in attendance. This historical event was proclaimed as the game of the century and was the forerunner for future NCAA championships to be held in domed stadiums.

It was a classic matchup of two future NBA stars, Elvin Hayes and Lew Alcindor (a/k/a Kareem Abdul-Jabbar). The massiveness of this crowd would influence many universities to build much larger arenas for their basketball teams. I sat on the edge of my seat, in awe of what was going on.

Two future Hall of Fame coaches, Johnny Wooden and Guy Lewis, pitted their two outstanding teams against each other. It was a great game, going right down to the wire with Houston prevailing 71 to 69. I left this game knowing full well that I had just witnessed the most unique sporting event in history.

The following week I was back to coaching my own team as we were in quest of a second consecutive state championship.

The second round of the district schedule started off just like the first as we won our first two games with ease. It had been such a long time since we were challenged that my guys were starting to get just a little bit cocky. When you basically blitz everybody on your schedule, it's hard not to be a little bit that way. I was constantly reminding my team that we were not close to being as good as we could be.

I wanted to keep them on their toes so they would never stop striving to improve. Our next game would be against Apple Springs. Their only loss in district was to us, so they were coming to Kennard with a chance for the district championship.

Our little gym was packed to the rafters and the atmosphere was extremely intense. After our last game, I was surprised that they chose to run with us because the fast-paced game was our strength. With the overflow crowd roaring about every basket and turnover, our full-court press was more than they could handle.

Balanced scoring would again describe our game as Roy and Butch scored 16 points apiece while Herman and Haywood got 12 and 11, respectively.

With this highly partisan, overflow home crowd igniting our game, we hustled our way to a 75-54 victory, thus becoming the District 45-B Champions.

After shaking hands with the Apple Springs players and coach, I walked back to the bench, picked up my clipboard and purple towel, and started for the dressing room. Before I left the gym, I saw Nelda rushing toward me.

The Pressing Champions

"Congratulations, Coach! District champs again. I'm so proud of you. If it wouldn't embarrass you, I'd like to give you a big hug right now."

"It's not going to embarrass me!"

She gave me a smile and a hug. Nelda turned out to be the Pied Piper because right behind her were the other cheerleaders—Carolyn Fowler, Mary Riley, and Betty Hammond, each delivering a congratulatory hug.

"Thanks, girls! I really appreciate what y'all do. Don't ever think that I don't notice what the cheerleaders do for our team."

They were all smiles as I headed for the dressing room, but before I got to the door, Nelda caught up with me to ask, "When are you going to have dinner with us again?"

"Next time I'm invited."

She walked away, then looked back and said, "I'll see what I can do about that."

I gave her a big smile and went into the dressing room.

Before practice the next day, I had the team sitting in the bleachers.

"First of all, I want to congratulate you guys again on winning the district championship. It's pretty obvious that we're the best team in the district. I'm just glad we've got an outstanding JV team to go against in practice. This not only prepared us for our district games, but it's building our team of the future.

"Secondly, I want to update you about next week. We'll have two warm-up games before the playoffs start. We have a game scheduled at Elkhart against Cayuga, the number one ranked team in East Texas."

Gary Parrish reacted to that news by asking, "Coach, you mean to tell me that these guys are ranked above us?"

"They are. They're an incredibly talented team with great size. We need to play a team like this. We need somebody that will challenge us because we haven't been challenged in a long time. That Elkhart gym will be rockin' because you'll have the best two teams in East Texas going against each other. The other game we have is with Central. I know we played them twice and beat them twice, but if you remember, after beating them badly the first time, they gave us all we wanted the second time.

"In their minds, they're thinking that they'll get us back this third time. Fellas, we've only had four games all year in which we were challenged and Central was one of those four. Besides, it's hard to beat your grandmother three times and that's what we're looking at with these guys. We need to be challenged and both of these games should give us that. Now, let's get to work and have a good practice. Let's warm up with five laps and then go to the star drill."

After running the 11-break drill for approximately twenty minutes, we shot free throws. We had six or seven players at each end of the floor with three or four balls at each basket. After each shot, I had the shooter walk to the other end, taking each step on the side of their foot. This was an ankle-strengthening exercise with each step putting your foot in the same position that happens when you turn an ankle. With each step, the weight of your body applies pressure on your ankle, strengthening this vulnerable area. I also had the guys waiting to shoot dribble the ball with their off hand. Essentially, we got three things done with each free-throw break.

Later, I had my team sitting in the bleachers talking about how important blocking out was.

"Look, Cayuga is much bigger than we are and if we don't do a great job of keeping them off the glass, it could be a real long night."

We had a hard practice and looked really good blocking out. I decided to cut practice a little shorter than normal. We've had so many hard, long practices this year it was time to back off a little bit to keep our legs fresh.

As I walked off the floor, Herman came up to me. In a quiet voice, he said, "Mom wants me to invite you to dinner tonight."

"Thanks, Herman. I'll be there shortly."

Sitting in my office, pondering today's practice, I thought to myself, *Nelda did not waste any time.*

The drive to Ratcliff only took a few minutes, barely enough time to listen to the Rolling Stones' new song "Jumping Jack Flash."

Coach Johnny Carter

Soon, I was knocking on the Myers' front door.

Nelda answered the door and welcomed me. "Come on in, Coach. Sure glad you could come. Make yourself at home. Herman and Jeff are watching TV. I've got to help Mom prepare dinner."

"Hey fellas, how's it going?" I said, walking into their family room.

Jeff looked up. "Have a seat, Coach."

"What are y'all watching?"

Herman took a sip of his iced tea, then said, "The Monkees."

Nelda came in from the kitchen and asked, "Would you like a glass of iced tea, Coach?"

"I would love a glass. Thanks Nelda."

Jeff asked, "Coach, tell us about Cayuga. They must be pretty good!"

"They're *really* good. They have great size and this will be the best rebounding team we've faced all year. If we don't somehow equalize their rebounding strength, we're looking at loss number two."

Herman said, "I can't wait to play them. Like you said, Coach, we need to play someone that challenges us."

"They will definitely do that."

Nelda returned and handed me a glass of tea. "They'd better be able to handle our press. That's the great equalizer. Y'all come to the table, supper's ready."

The Pressing Champions

Sitting around the dinner table a little later, I looked at Mrs. Myers. "I really appreciate y'all inviting me for dinner. Boy, does that look good."

"Coach, I hope you like chicken fried steak."

"Love it," I replied.

As we were enjoying a wonderful meal, Harley Myers said, "I love that pressing defense. I've never seen a Kennard team play that hard in all my years here."

"Thanks, I really appreciate that. We seem to be getting better with it every day. It didn't happen overnight, though. It took many long hours of practice."

Mrs. Myers said, "Coach, it's amazing what you've accomplished in the short time you've been here. I'm not talking just about basketball. Integration hasn't even been an issue and I think you're one of the main reasons why."

"I don't know about that. It could be because the community is unified in pulling for our basketball team. I wonder how it would be if our basketball team wasn't very good."

Nelda spoke up. "I think it's because everyone sees how good your players get along with each other and it carries over to everyone else."

I smiled at her remark.

"When teammates genuinely care for each other, it brings about togetherness, which leads to unity and triggers success. That's the main reason why our team has done so well."

Coach Johnny Carter

Herman added, "It helps when the team looks up to and believes in their coach."

"Thanks, Herman. I really appreciate that. Wow! Would you look at the time! I need to go because I've got to prepare a science test for tomorrow. Thank you so much for inviting me. The meal was fabulous."

Nelda smiled. "Thanks for coming. I really enjoyed you being here. We'll have to do this again sometime."

"I'm already looking forward to it."

Chapter 9
Cayuga

An overflow crowd filled the Elkhart gym to capacity as we hoped to extend our 33-game winning streak. Cayuga had a rich history of producing great high school basketball teams, having previously won three state championships.

Two of those championships came under the direction of Joe Turner, legendary Kilgore Junior College coach. Shelby Metcalf, the longtime head coach at Texas A&M began his coaching career here. He would become the longest-serving basketball coach (26 years) in Southwest Conference history. This was also the home of one of my childhood SMU heroes—Ned Duncan.

With an outstanding basketball legacy, the number one ranked Class A team in East Texas compiling a record of 29-1 was about to face off against our Tigers, the number 1 ranked Class B team at 37-1.

This was the game that everyone wanted to see, a match-up between two teams that had completely dominated the opposition all year.

As we warmed up, Walter Denman looked at me and said, "Coach, compared to us, those guys are huge!"

I smiled. "Have we ever had a height advantage?"

As Richard Curry came by, he asked, "So what's new, Coach?"

Coach Johnny Carter

Eddie Ray Pilkington chimed in, "Games like this are what all those weight vest workouts were for, right Coach?"

I smiled as the buzzer sounded to start the game. Our intense full-court pressure defense paid big time dividends early as we build up a 20-9 lead in the first quarter. However, midway through the second quarter, Butch Walker got his third foul and had to come to the bench.

At that point, the game changed as Cayuga's height advantage took center stage. Led by Clarence Dawson's 19 points, the game went right down to the final seconds with Cayuga squeaking out a 54-52 victory.

The atmosphere in the dressing room was downcast. I did my best to put a positive spin on the outcome.

"Look, I'm very proud of your effort out there tonight. We played a very good team and we definitely needed a game like this. Sometimes, even when you give it all you have, things don't work out. We held our own out there tonight and the game could've gone either way.

About this time last year, we lost a warm-up game and what happened? We won the state championship.

So, get your heads up and let this loss be a springboard for a bigger and better future. Hey, win or lose, I will always love you guys. Let's go home."

That loss indeed motivated us and proved to be a wake-up call, thus intensifying our game. Our practices reflected this as it did in our next game. The victim would be Central as we blitzed them 70-48 in our last warm-up game before the playoffs.

With our four seniors all scoring in double figures (Herman 18, Haywood 17, Roy 16, and Nubbin 11), we completely dominated a team we'd beaten by only four points earlier. Led by Tommy Luce, Rayford Quine, and Carroll Richardson, Central was also headed for the playoffs and would have to be reckoned with.

Chapter 10
The Playoffs

The third season, the playoff season, was staring us right in the face. By going undefeated in the district race and then splitting two warm-up games, we were looking at several similarities to last year.

One year ago, we lost a warm up game after a long winning streak. That loss took away the slight cockiness that was developing, triggered a new intensity, and sent us to bi-district with a lot to prove.

In essence, that's exactly what was going on right now. Just like last year, our first playoff game would be played in Madisonville after already having played four tournament games there. I was hoping that we would play as well this year because last year we had one of our best games of the year, winning that first playoff game.

Our opponent this year would be Iola High School from the same district that Anderson won last year. They had an outstanding record of 20-5 having beaten some outstanding teams and would be a very formidable opponent. Several years later, this school would produce a future NBA player. Chris "Birdman" Anderson would play pro basketball for numerous years, winning an NBA championship with the Miami Heat in 2013.

If our rejuvenated intensity in practice was any indication, we appeared to be ready for that game;

The Pressing Champions

however, practice is practice and there's no way to create total game-like conditions. A lot of teams have great practices and think they're ready for the big game, but until you put that uniform on, come out of the dressing room before a packed house, and have that opening tip, then and only then do you find out if you're actually ready!

Illustration by my son, John Carter

We arrived in Madisonville before the big game and stopped at my parents' home for a little pre-game pick me up of hot tea (with lemon and honey.)

My mom and dad loved having our team stop by their home and my guys definitely felt at home there. Mom had prepared the tea and Dad was talking to all the players, encouraging them. Dad asked me earlier if there was anything he could do to help prepare for this game. I told him to just spread the word about it. I think he did more than that because when we got to the gym, it looked like half of Madisonville was in the stands.

When you couple that with all the fans from Houston County, just like last year, we definitely had the support of the majority of the crowd. That gave us a huge advantage and it showed when the game started. We started the game with a bang, outscoring the Bulldogs 23-6 in the first quarter. Our pressure defense was too much for Iola and we went on to a 91-52 victory.

Again, we had a great balanced scoring attack as all five starters scored in double figures. Ray Pointer was the leading scorer for Iola with 19. Brown and McDonald had 10 points apiece. We duplicated last year's bi-district performance with one of our best games of the year and would be heading to the regional tournament with a positive mindset.

Haywood, who always seemed to have a positive attitude anyway, came up to me in the dressing room with a sly smile on his face. "Coach, we played good, I mean *real* good! You know...I don't know if we can play any better than that."

With a raised eyebrow and a slight smile starting to come, I looked at Haywood, who was already smiling, almost laughing. We both looked at each other and said in unison, "WE CAN ALWAYS PLAY BETTER!"

Heading down Highway 7 through the pines, I stopped by the school to get a cup of coffee on my way to

The Pressing Champions

Kilgore and the regional tournament meeting. Sitting with Curtis, Benford, and Miss Nona, it was all basketball talk about how well we played last night.

Never known for not having something to say or give an opinion, Benford looked at me and said, "Well, Coach, last night it was like last year all over again. We jumped on those guys at the start and they really never had a chance. Congratulations!

"Coach, I see once again that there'll be an uneven number of teams at the tournament." He looked at me and laughed. "I've got it all figured out, so here's the plan. Just go on up to Kilgore and draw that bye again, so maybe, just maybe we'll be back in Austin next week!"

With a hint of sarcasm, I said, "I like the way you're thinking and you know what…that's exactly what I plan to do!"

Illustration by my son, John Carter

Chapter 11
The Regional Tournament

With the backdrop of historic oil derricks checkerboarding the landscape along the way, I soon was driving through downtown Kilgore. When oil was discovered

The Pressing Champions

here some 38 years ago, this area became the largest concentration of oil wells in the world.

It was also right here one year ago when I reached in the hat and pulled out a rabbit, getting the coveted bye in the first round. *Could that happen again? No way,* I thought.

Looking around the room, there were some familiar faces from last year. A few minutes later, Joe Turner, head coach and athletic director at Kilgore Junior College, entered the room.

After explaining the tournament format, he looked around the room and said, "If there are no questions, let's find out the match-ups in the first round."

Like last year, I was the first coach to reach into the hat. *What are the odds of drawing that bye two years in a row?* My eyes almost popped out of my head when I opened up that piece of paper because there it was—lucky number seven, AGAIN!

For the second straight year, I'd once again defied all odds by getting an automatic first round victory. In my mind, I looked to the heavens, thanking the Lord for another extremely special gift. I was elated. It seemed like I was re-living last year all over again.

As I exited the meeting, one of the older coaches looked at me and said, "Coach, you seem to have all the luck on your side. If you ever go to Las Vegas, let me know!"

I smiled at him and said, "It wasn't luck, it was a true blessing."

As I drove back through the East Texas oil fields on my way home, I couldn't help but think about how this year resembled a mirror image of last year. All the similarities were there.

When I got back to the school, I couldn't wait to tell Miss Nona of our good fortune. "Coach, you must be living right! That's amazing!"

Later, in practice, just like last year, my players were ecstatic when I told them the news.

Herman Myers' face was beaming. "Coach, this is unreal! How did you do that two years in a row?"

I smiled at him and the rest of the team, pointed upward and said, "We are blessed."

I told them what the plans were for the next three days. "We'll have two practices today and tomorrow. On Friday, I'll be going up to Kilgore to scout and find out who we play.

"We won't have an after-school practice on Friday. I want you guys last period to have an informal shoot-around, work on jumpers and free throws, and go home with the bell. We'll leave early Saturday morning and play two games at Kilgore, just like last year."

After warming up, I called the team over to the side and said, "I think all of you know what to do on our 2-2-1 press, but the next two days we're going to work hard on running that when we don't score and at the same time, running our regular full-court press when we do.

"Okay, let's run our offense and see how fast we can get into these two different presses."

We'd worked on both of these presses a lot, but most of the time we ran them separately. Since most of our district games were blowouts, we used the half-court press only when the game was pretty much out of hand, just to work on it. Our only two losses of the year were the result of poor shooting, which gave us less full-court press opportunities.

Looking back, we could've very well won both of those games had we used the half-court press on missed baskets. This half-court press could be a lifesaver if we did have another one of those kinds of games. I really liked what I saw because this would give us a chance to apply pressure all the time.

Curtis and I were in the stands in Kilgore, scouting the three regional preliminary games.

"Well, Coach, here we are again, just like last year, getting to scout all the teams that we might play tomorrow. Getting that bye again was such an advantage!"

Redwater was impressive as they soundly defeated Eustace 88–68.

In analyzing our Saturday morning opponent, Curtis said, "Boy, that Larry Stinson is some kind of a player.

We've got to figure out some way to stop him, Coach, because he can carry that team by himself."

In the other two first round games, Chester, which might be a team of the future, upset Woden. Frankston came from behind in the closing minutes to defeat Carlisle.

Our first-round opponent at Regional would be Redwater, a small community twelve miles southwest of Texarkana in far northeast Texas. Early on, it was basically a sawmill town which grew up in the 1870s. During World War II, the Red River Army Depot and Lone Star Army Ammunition Plant were built just north of Redwater. This plant, which provided thousands of jobs, produced ammunition for World War II, the Korean War, and the Vietnam war.

Saturday morning, I stood before my team in the dressing room at Masters Gym on the campus of Kilgore Junior College.

"You're about to go against a team that scored 88 points last night. They're red hot! It's up to you to cool them off! They're highly ranked. They've won 31 games this year. Their best player is Larry Stinson, who averages over 20 points a game. They're much more than a one-dimensional team as they have several guys who can score. This is one of the best teams that we'll play all year, so we need to get after them early. Let's get off to a great start and give them a negative mindset right off the bat."

The Pressing Champions

We did indeed come out of the gate full blast and with the press again paying big dividends, we led 37-26 at the half.

Continuing to play well, we increased our lead by 14 starting the fourth quarter. The game changed dramatically when Haywood and Butch had to go to the bench with four fouls.

Redwater then began a ferocious comeback with Stinson, Eddie Bell, and Bill Cooper leading the charge. Forced to put Haywood and Butch back in the game, I was attempting to derail this comeback before it slipped away. Redwater had a ton of momentum and when Haywood fouled out, it gave them more confidence. Butch Walker had played a great game scoring 21 points, but he also had to leave the game with five fouls. Now the Dragons were breathing fire and they could smell a come-from-behind victory.

They cut the lead to 3 with 7 seconds left when Larry Stinson was fouled. He made the first free-throw to cut the lead to 65-63. I called timeout. Looking into the faces of my shell-shocked team, I went over the situation.

"Look, he may try to miss this free-throw on purpose and if he does, we must get the rebound. Remember all the times we've worked on the defensive free-throw situation. You two guys on top – one of you block out the shooter and the other go right down the middle for the rebound. If he makes the free-throw, we're still one point ahead. If that happens, Roy, I want you to take the ball out of bounds, run hard toward the right, fake a pass and then run hard to your left and look for Herman when he comes off that pick from Nubbin. They're probably going to foul you, Herman. That's okay, you make the free throws it's over anyway. Look, we have one timeout left, so if you get in trouble, use it."

There was a lot of nervous tension in the air as this game was about to be decided in those last crucial seconds. Larry Stinson had played one great game, scoring 21 points. When he purposely missed his second free-throw, we failed to execute what I'd said in the timeout because the ball bounced right back to him with a chance to tie the score.

Everyone was standing, holding their breath as he took the shot that would've brought them all the way back. Fortunately for us, it failed to connect. Herman got the rebound and was immediately fouled with two seconds left. Our crowd let out a sigh of relief as Herman went to the foul line and calmly sank two free throws for a 67–63 victory.

All year long I was concerned about the fact that we had very few close games. Reacting and winning a game under this kind of adverse circumstances was huge. We'd just dodged a bullet and we were happy to get out of the gym with a victory. When you have two of your best players on the bench, the fact that we survived was a true test of our depth.

As I walked off the floor, my dad came up to me. With a relieved look on his face, he said, "You know, son, good teams figure out a way to win, even when things don't go

The Pressing Champions

as planned. You did that today. Congratulations! It wasn't pretty, but we'll take it. A win is a win! Now go in there and congratulate your guys because you've got an even bigger game coming up tonight."

As I walked to the dressing room, I was thinking that this is the first game we've had like this all year, with the exception of the Cayuga game. We lost that one. We had a big lead in that game only to see them come back strong and pull out a victory. Today's game was very similar to that contest, only this one was much more important.

We managed to hold off a red-hot team and won the game despite having two of our best players on the bench. This was a positive and exactly the way I approached my team in the dressing room.

Curtis and I sat in the bleachers and watched Frankston play Chester in the other semi-final game. We had convincingly defeated Frankston right here on this floor last year, but they appeared to be a much better team now. Their two best players, David Coker and Cole Pugh, were returning starters from last year. Chester had the height and some excellent young players. Frankston's experience proved to be the difference and they went on to win this game 70–62.

The regional final game would be a rematch with Frankston, attempting to erase the memory of that loss to us last year. They would be highly motivated for that fact alone and, like everyone else, they wanted to knock off last year's state champion.

"What do you think, Curtis?"

"We snuck up on them last year. That won't happen this year. They're much better, but then so are we. They're polished, make very few mistakes, and are very good shooters. We'll have to be on top of our game or it could be a long night."

In fact, Frankston, under the direction of veteran coach, Bo Ousley, had established a legacy of winning basketball. They were consistently in the regional tournament and had previously won a state championship in 1961. Mike Cook, one of my best friends and teammates, played on that team. We shared many high school memories while playing basketball together at Lon Morris Junior College.

Chapter 12
The Regional Finals

We had rented a couple of hotel rooms for our guys to rest up between games. When you play two games of this significance in the same day, it's extremely important to refresh yourself and get your legs ready for the second game. After all, this was for the regional championship and that coveted trip to the state tournament, something every high school player with a passion for the sport has dreams of doing.

It's a game, particularly when you're a senior, when it's your last hurrah. Having played in that game and lost, then watched my brother's team do the same, it's devastating and hard to get past. It's difficult to sit in the stands in Austin and watch the team that barely beat you easily win the state championship. You don't get over that overnight.

Tonight, one team will be headed to Austin, hoping for a state championship while the other will go home with a shattered dream. Walter Cronkite, longtime anchor of the CBS evening news had a favorite quote which I always liked. "And that's the way it is."

After our pre-game meal, we headed back to Masters Gym for the regional championship game.

In the dressing room, prior to the game, I addressed my team.

Coach Johnny Carter

"Frankston is a much better team than they were last year and they've got more than one reason to try and beat us. They're well coached and I have a lot of respect for Bo Ousley. We know about Pugh and Coker from last year, but don't neglect Joe Ellis, Mike Bird, and John Coleman.

"We've worked real hard this year to run our defenses and not get in foul trouble. Tonight, we've got to play smart defensively. I don't want to see any of you guys get your tail in foul trouble again!

"Look, I think that you're a better team than they are, but you have to go out there and prove it. They're not going to lay down because we're the defending state champion. We're going to start off with our full-court press on made baskets and the half-court trap when we don't score. I think this is a perfect game plan for tonight because Frankston plays pretty deliberate. You should have no trouble setting up the 2-2-1 after a missed basket. The key to this game is pressure defense and if you can create a lot of turnovers, you're gonna win this game!

"Oh, one more thing. The only team that beat Cayuga this year is the team we're just about to play.

"Any questions? Okay, everybody, grab a knee. Let's have our prayer."

The game started and the Frankston Indians immediately took control, hitting an exceptional high percentage of their shots. Meanwhile, we couldn't throw

The Pressing Champions

one in the ocean. We hit a miserable one for 23 at the game's outset, trailing 12-3 at the end of the first quarter, by far our least productive quarter for the entire year. We were in trouble, big time trouble.

Our poor shooting had given them a boatload of confidence and our mindset at the present was in the gutter. We were facing a red-hot team that appeared to be destined to avenge their loss to us in the regional last year.

While facing an Indian rampage of epic proportion, we had no other choice, at least early on, but to circle the wagons because they were in total control. Our full-court press was virtually nonexistent because you have to score to get into it. The only bright spot was we were running the 2-2-1 after missed baskets and this absolutely saved us early on. We did force several turnovers which limited their number of offensive possessions, thus keeping us within possible striking distance. This half-court trap literally was the only positive for our team in the first quarter. Without it, this game might very well be out-of-control.

It appeared that the second quarter would be just like the first as we hit only one basket in the first five minutes. I couldn't help but think that our very close morning game with Redwater had taken some of the sap out of us. Then Herman hit a jumper, igniting our full-court press. Nubbin immediately stole the inbounds pass, hit Butch for a free throw line jumper and, in a flash, momentum was on our side, at least temporarily. This carried us the rest of the half as we ended up with 23 points and cut their lead to four at the break.

In the third quarter, Haywood got his third foul. A couple of minutes later, the referee blew his whistle charging Roy with his third. Our crowd was sitting on their hands, stunned at what was going on. That's when my dad went into action.

Arrow points to my Dad who is rousing fans to keep cheering

Sitting on the front row, he stood up, hat in hand and began a whirlybird motion to the crowd. All of a sudden, he pretty much single-handedly got the crowd back into the game. To say this crowd reaction fired us up would be an understatement. I was in the process of taking Haywood out when he got his fourth foul. I decided to put Lester Hutcherson in the game and he promptly hit a basket, giving my sophomore leading scorer on the JV a lot of confidence.

We trailed by six at the end of the third quarter. In the huddle, I tried really hard to pump up our confidence.

"If you're ever going to give it all you've got, it's gotta start right now. We've come too far to give up now!"

At that moment, I reminded myself of a Bible verse, second Chronicles 15:7, which says, "But as for you, be strong and do not give up, for your work will be rewarded."

In an emotional, raised voice, I said, "This fourth quarter belongs to us! It's our time! Now go out there and take this thing!"

We started whittling away as the press gave us a quick basket, but then Roy over-playing on defense got his fourth foul. It would be very hard for Roy and Haywood to play the rest of this game without fouling out. I was worried about this because these two guys were so important in our overall game.

During a timeout, I looked into the faces of these two young men and said, "You've got to play smart. We need you in this game."

It's extremely hard to play with four fouls, particularly when you're pressing. I have to give the Indians credit because they were facing a ferocious full-court press and so far had handled it fairly well.

Then, just as I feared, with 3:34 left in the game, Haywood, playing intense pressure defense, got his fifth foul. Many of our fans thought this was the final nail in our coffin.

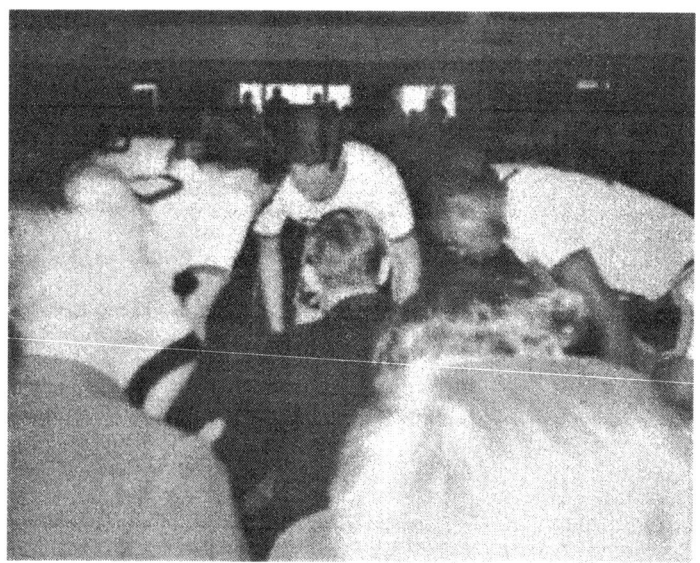

"Don't give up!"

Chapter 13
Saved by a Sophomore

As I walked down the front of the bench, I had a sinking feeling in the pit of my stomach. I looked at each player and that uneasy air of obvious negativity engulfed our bench.

Nobody looked like they wanted to go in until I got to Lester. This wiry sophomore had a very positive look on his face as he raised his hand, indicating to me that he was the guy. It took me about one second to decide to put him in the game. This turned out to be the most important substitution that I'd made all year.

Lester Hutcherson

Almost immediately, Lester hit a quick basket. A little over a minute later, Roy fouled out, instantly swinging the momentum back to Frankston. We were now in dire straits and many of our fans thought this was the last straw. Some walked toward the exits.

I put in Jeff Myers, our freshman JV point guard. He immediately got the ball to Lester.

Coach Johnny Carter

With ice water in his veins, my rising sophomore executed a nice crossover dribble and then with a quick wrist flip, put up a soft jumper that became a rotating rainbow right toward the rim. The Kennard crowd was standing and praying for a basket.

They soon got their answer. Echoing in the background, the PA announcer said, "Basket by Hutcherson."

It was Lester's third basket of the evening, cutting their lead to three. The Indians were really feeling the pressure now as Nubbin stole the ball and then rifled a quick pass to Lester.

With a rocker step and a nice pump fake, he put up a soft spinner that curled around the rim before gently stretching the strings and dropping to the floor.

Demonstrating that he belonged in the game at this time, Lester had just hit his third consecutive big shot, amazingly his fourth off-the-bench crunch-time clutch basket of the evening.

Our crowd was delirious as we were surging, while slicing Frankston's narrow lead to just one point. Most of those who had left early were now rushing back to their seats, hoping for a frantic photo finish.

Frankston was on their heels and could feel this one slipping away. Butch Walker had played a great game and with 2:08 left he put up a turnaround, soft spinning jumper that ripped the cords, giving us the lead for the first time in the game. The very partisan crowd on our

The Pressing Champions

side exploded with a roaring, roof-raising rapid response. That basket gave Butch 21 points for the night.

Not ready to give up, Cole Pugh, going for his 17th point, promptly hit a short jumper to put the Indians right back up by one; however, with 1:21 left in the game, he fouled out.

Herman then went to the foul line, calmly flipped the wrist with the first of two free-throws. As the arched trajectory headed toward the goal, the crowd anxiously awaited this nail-biter moment and then there it was, nothing but net. It had been a long, hard, uphill battle, but now, for the first time since the opening tip, the score was tied, igniting a massive volcano-like eruption from our crowd.

With Herman's second free throw, he was going for his 22nd point of the night. He eyed the basket, took a deep breath, dribbled the ball three times, and with perfect form, bent his knees, flipped his wrist, and followed through. With the crowd collectively holding its breath, his arched, spinning shot spiraled through the air. When it reached the rim, there it was, that successful sweet silent sound. SWISH! Our crowd's spontaneous, thunderous reaction was automatic, igniting a bombastic blast of deafening approval.

Herman's two free throws had put us ahead for keeps, sending us to a 64–63 amazing come-from-behind victory. Just like last year, we had a great comeback, winning by just one point.

Coach Johnny Carter

Lester came up to me, smiled that beautiful big smile, and said, "Coach, we're going back to Austin!"

I took one look at him, gave him a big hug, and said, "Thanks to you, son! You were the difference tonight!"

Coming off the bench with a ton of pressure on his back, this slender sophomore more than came through in the clutch in undoubtedly the biggest game of the year. Looking back on the year, I was always worried about the fact that we had so many games that were blowouts and rather than just run the score up, I worked in some of the young guys just to get valuable experience in varsity games. Tonight, that paid off in a big way because Lester didn't act like he was a bench player. He looked like one of our best players. In leading our JV team to a 19-2 record, I was already impressed with him, but tonight put his value to a new level.

Pandemonium again reigned supreme that cool February night in this historic oil field city. Again, I was mobbed by our cheerleaders. Nelda looked at me and said, "You're amazing coach! Two years in a row and again we're Austin bound!"

My dad came up to me, gave me a hug and said, "Congratulations, son! You overcame incredible adversity tonight and your team never gave up."

Emotionally overwhelmed, I looked at Dad. "You NEVER gave up either, Dad and you NEVER let our crowd give up. Thanks."

The Pressing Champions

Mom also gave me a hug and told me how she'd been praying hard. My brother, James Otis smiled and shook my hand.

"You always said that in order to get to the top you'll have at least one game where everything goes wrong and you've still got to figure out a way to win. Well, that's exactly what you guys did tonight. There's something extra special about this team. They just refuse to lose. Congratulations!"

As the defending state champion now, thanks to an incredible never-give-up effort, we showed a lot of HEART and now had a new lease on life—a chance to repeat. Many years later, after winning a second straight NBA championship, Rudy Tomjanovich, head coach of the Houston Rockets, made a profound statement that I hoped applied here:

"Never under estimate the heart of a champion."

As I shook hands with all the players and Coach Ousley, I couldn't help but feel for them. I'd already experienced this when I played and as I looked in their eyes, I could definitely identify with their feelings. They'd played a near-perfect game, shot an incredible 60% from the field, hit a high percentage of their free throws, rebounded well, had great balanced scoring with four players in double figures, and they totally had us on the ropes until the last two minutes.

Coach Johnny Carter

There was one big negative that caused them to lose this game and that was turnovers. Our pressure defense forced over twenty turnovers which literally kept us in the game. Were it not for that one statistic, they would have easily won. It was about this time last year in the regional final when we had to use the full-court press late to come from behind, defeating Avinger. The impact of this game is when I decided to build my future teams around the press. If we hadn't changed our style of play this year in going to full-court pressure defense, Frankston would be going to Austin.

Later, we were headed home, I couldn't help but reminisce. Two years in a row we had played for the regional championship at Masters Gym and won them both with comeback one-point victories. I thought to myself *Wow! What special memories. There's no way to ever top this."*

Little did I realize that about ten years later I would return to this same gym as the head coach at McLennan Community College in Waco and coach the highest scoring game in the history of basketball, defeating Kilgore Junior College 169–165 in four overtimes.

This incredible game would be Paul Harvey's lead story on his syndicated coast-to-coast news broadcast. Later, the game ball would be placed in the trophy case at the National Basketball Hall of Fame in Springfield, Massachusetts.

The Pressing Champions

The trip back from Kilgore was a joyful journey and seemed to go much quicker than the trip there. Nevertheless, it was in the wee hours of the morning when we finally arrived home.

What a day it had been. We had survived two pressure-packed games and again would be headed to Austin. I'd planned to stop by my apartment in Crockett and then driving on to Madisonville, but I never made it. I made the mistake of lying down and was so physically, mentally and emotionally exhausted, I fell sound asleep.

When I woke up, it was Sunday morning. Soon on the road, I arrived in Madisonville just a little bit late for the 11 o'clock service at the First Methodist Church. I knew I wasn't too late though, because opening the door right behind me was Buddy Barrett. He was known to occasionally be late for church, but was always there.

He reached out, shook my hand, and said, "Well, Johnny, two years, two state tournaments, is there any better way to start a coaching career?"

"I don't think so, but I've been real lucky, Buddy."

"It takes a lot more than luck to do what you've done."

With an appreciative smile, I entered the church.

After the service, the first two guys to congratulate me were Jerry Reed and John Hardy, two local businessmen.

Jerry looked at me and said somewhat sarcastically, "Do you ever lose a big game?"

I chuckled. "I haven't coached long enough."

John gave me a sly smile and said, "It's going to be awfully hard to keep up this pace."

I rolled my eyes and nodded my head in total agreement. Two local dentists, my uncle, Jeff Carter and Butch Bennett, also offered their congratulations.

Butch said, "You were a fierce competitor when you played, but not nearly as competitive as you are as a coach."

"Speaking of competitive, you were one of the most competitive players I ever faced!"

Butch smiled as two brothers, Sam and P.M. Standley, walked up to me.

"Have you guys got your reservations yet?"

"Johnny," Sam replied, "you know we never miss the state tournament. We'll be there rooting you on again. Good luck."

After a wonderful day with my family, I spent the night and then drove back to school on Monday morning. The air was crisp this late February, early spring morning.

As I walked down the hall toward the cafeteria, no less than ten kids walked up and offered congratulations. When I reached the cafeteria door, Gary Parrish and Clayton Baker stopped me.

Gary looked at Clayton and then at me. "Can you believe we won that game?"

The Pressing Champions

"Statistically, there was no way, but you know statistics don't measure what's inside the heart," I replied. "All I can say is thank goodness for our pressing defense. It saved us. Clayton, you kept the stats, what do you think?"

Clayton smiled. "I was sitting right there on the bench beside you and I still can't believe it happened."

Lester Hutcherson, my slender sophomore, was coming down the hall proudly wearing his state champion letter jacket.

Clayton stopped mid-sentence and said, "Here comes one of the main reasons we won!"

"Congratulations, son!" I said reaching out to shake Lester's hand. "The attacking Indians were on the warpath and it looked like we were done for, but then you came riding in like John Wayne and the U.S. Cavalry and sent them right back to the reservation."

Lester gave me a big, yet modest smile.

"By the way, I ordered that other patch that you said you wanted for your letter jacket."

Lester looked puzzled until I said, "Are you sure all you want it to say is HERO?"

Now we were all laughing as I walked into the cafeteria.

Benford Frizzell walked up to me and said, "Now that's what I call some real ball coaching!"

Curtis walked in and joined in our conversation.

"Well, Coach, if anybody has any doubts about our full-court press, they needed to watch that game because without it we wouldn't be laughing right now. Frankston would be going to state and our season would be over."

Miss Nona smiled and asked, "What did you feed Lester before that game? It was unreal what he did!" With a laugh and a keen understanding of what happened, Benford said, "Are you sure he's just a sophomore because he sure didn't play like one!"

Chapter 14
Austin, here we are again!

With a whirlwind of activity, we got all the details worked out and we were on our way to Austin for an attempt at repeating last year's state championship victory. With most of our team returning from last year, only James Smith and Richard Curry were making this trip for the first time and it would be extra special for them.

Unlike last year when we were just glad to be making the trip to Austin, this year we were going there to win. Before the regional tournament, we thought that we were the best team in the state and after two cliffhangers, we now had a chance to prove that we were.

After checking into the Stephen F Austin Hotel and settling in, we were now ready to resume our quest for a second straight state championship.

It was Wednesday morning and every team that qualified for the state tournament was allotted 30 minutes of shooting time in Gregory Gym the day before the state tournament started. We arrived at the gym about 15 minutes prior to our practice time.

When we got there, I was greeted by my junior college coach, Leon Black, who was now the head coach at the University of Texas.

Coach Johnny Carter

"Hello Johnny! Congratulations! You survived that Kilgore region again. That's quite an accomplishment in itself!"

"Thanks Coach, we're fortunate to be here."

"Well, last year you were the underdog. How does it feel to be the favorite?"

"We were a total unknown last year and now everybody's trying to knock us off. The surprise element is no longer in our description. We now have to approach every game knowing that the team we play is probably going to play way above their head. In fact, that's already happened many times this year."

"Unfortunately, that comes with the territory," Coach Black replied.

About that time, Jim O'Bannon, Coach Black's assistant, walked up, gestured to me, and said, "This guy doesn't think there's anything to it!"

Our first-round opponent on Thursday morning was Prairie Valley High School from Nocona. Located near the Oklahoma border, this town's name came from a Comanche Indian chief and is also the original home of the well-known Nocona Boot Company.

One of its famous residents was Charlie Robertson, a professional baseball pitcher for the Chicago White Sox.

In 1922, going against future Hall of Famer, Ty Cobb and the Detroit Tigers, he pitched a perfect game, one of only 23 perfect games in the history of Major League

The Pressing Champions

Baseball. After this miraculous accomplishment, 34 years would pass until this very rare achievement happened again. Growing up a White Sox fan, I found this very interesting.

Illustration by my son, John Carter

Charlie Robertson
1922 Chicago White Sox

Coach Johnny Carter

Chapter 15
State '68

The Prairie Valley Bulldogs, coached by Tom Foster, were making their fifth trip to the state tournament. Their impressive record was 33-6. They had handily defeated some very good teams, including Krum, the team that we squeaked by last year in the state championship game. Statistically, they looked very similar to our team. The average points per game and points given up were almost identical.

The Pressing Champions

Individually, they had three players averaging in double figures: Wayne Sappington and Sam Thompkins averaged 17 points apiece, while Steve Brown was at 15. We had four: Herman 17, Roy 16, Haywood 14, Butch 12, and when you consider that Nubbin averaged nine, we were close to having five. Statistics are fine to read, but they don't really mean a hill of beans because once you throw the ball up, it's all about what your team does that day.

As we warmed up prior to the start of this game, two guys sitting right in front of Curtis commented about our team. One of them, who was obviously unimpressed with the way our team looked, made a sarcastic comment.

"I can't believe that little team even made it to the state tournament. How the heck did those guys even get up here? I've seen Prairie Valley play and they're fixing to kick Kennard's butt."

When the game started, we came out of the starting blocks full blast, totally dominating the first half. Our pressure defense was superb, forcing 14 turnovers while only having two of our own. We built up a huge 46-20 lead.

When we walked off the floor at the half, that same unimpressed guy said, "I see now why that team is up here! They're pretty good!"

The other guy's facial expression said it all. "No, not *pretty* good...they're *real* good! Curtis wanted to say something to them, but instead he just laughed.

Coach Johnny Carter

The second half was an exact replica of the first and we ended up with an overwhelming 92-52 win. Butch had a great game, scoring 24 points and pulling down 17 rebounds. This was a near-perfect, beautifully balanced team effort as the rest of the team also played extremely well, with Haywood scoring 21, Herman and Roy at 17 points apiece and Nubbin coming in with 11.

When you have all five starters scoring in double digits, that's about as good as it gets. The 92 points set a new state tournament Class B scoring record, besting Snook's previous record of 89 points in 1965.

There's nothing like the positive vibes coming from a dressing room when your team has had a great game. Butch came up to me, gave me a big handshake and said, "How about that game, Coach!"

"How about those rebounds, Butch! You got a bunch, great job!"

Knowing that he'd played a very good game, he acknowledged the praise with a big smile.

Walter Denman looked at me and said, "Coach, that's got to be our best game of the year."

Looking up from untying his shoelaces, Leeland Strban said, "I agree with Walter. We did everything well today."

Eddie Pilkington walked over to me and said, "Well, what do you think, Coach?"

"I don't know if it's our best, but it's definitely one of our best. We had a great combination of offense and defense today, because we scored over 20 points above our average and held them to 20 points below theirs. That's a difference of 40 points. We made a pretty good team look pretty bad. They're a much better team than they showed today."

Roy said, "Our defense just got into their heads, Coach. We made a lot of good teams look bad this year. I'm sure that they're a lot better than they played today, but you know something, Coach, I don't know if we can play any better than we did today."

Roy and I looked at each other, both smiling, and in unison with the rest of the team said, "WE CAN ALWAYS PLAY BETTER!"

Coming out of the dressing room, I was met by reporters Tommy Anderson of the *Austin American Statesman* and David Weidner of the *Lufkin News*.

David asked me if I was surprised that we were 22 points above our points-per-game average today.

"Not really…I guess the main reason is because my first team is playing more minutes in these very important games than in the regular season. I don't like to run up the score on people, but when I was told that we were real close to breaking the record, I decided to let our team go for it."

I was then asked to compare last year's state championship team with this year's team.

"I don't really like to compare teams because every year and every team is different; however, because of the different style of play that we've employed this year, we're probably 15–20 points a game better this year. I love full-court pressure defense, our players are absolutely sold on it and with the big change in the style of play, we're getting a lot more shots every game. It stands to reason that we're scoring a lot more points."

"Coach, your team had all five starters in double figures today. Does that happen very often?" Tommy asked.

I explained to him that it does happen quite often. "This is one of the main reasons why our team did so well this year. You can't just key on any one player, you've got to guard them all. I absolutely love that about our team. We are well-balanced, confident, and I hope it will last for two more games."

"One last thing, Coach," Dave said. "You play Leuders-Avoca in the semifinals tomorrow. What do you know about them?"

"They have a very good team. They're 37-3 and are well coached. Clayton Brooks is an outstanding coach. Their two best players are probably James Creel and Larry Rister. Looks like we've got our work cut out for us. We played them last year up here. Ironically, at that time they were the favorite, averaging close to 80 points a game. Our goal was to slow them down and hold them below their average. We did that, held them to 32 points below their average and won the game.

"Now we're the favorite and our style of play is totally reversed from last year because now we're

The Pressing Champions

running, pressing, and capable of scoring lots of points. I don't think they'll try to slow us down because they're a team that also likes to run, but if they do, we'll adjust to it. So, if they decide to run with us, it should be an entertaining game."

Later, while visiting with my family, my dad gave me his opinion of the game. "I've seen most of our games this year and I believe that's the best you guys have played all year. I can't think of one facet of our game that didn't look superb. I don't see how we can play much better than that."

I smiled as I put my index finger to my lips.

"I agree, but please don't tell my players that. As long as we have a game left, I don't ever want them to think that they can't improve."

My brother Billy looked at me and said, "Man, Butch played well today! How long has he been playing like that?"

"He's really come on strong the last couple of weeks. He had an absolutely great regional tournament and his improvement has made our team better."

My brother James Otis smiled. "You keep playing like that and nobody here is gonna touch you."

"I hope you're right. I'm taking my team to have lunch in about 15 minutes. You guys are welcome to come if you want."

Coach Johnny Carter

As I was hurrying down the steps of Gregory gym, I heard somebody in the background hollering, "Wait up, Johnny!"

It was Tommy Ferguson, my very good friend, former teammate, and classmate at Madisonville.

"Man, Johnny, you guys played great today! There must've been some tough teams at regional because you had a couple of super close games."

"Yeah, we had two nail-biters that could've gone either way. You know how regional can be. Many times, it's a lot tougher than the state tournament and this year was no exception."

"You must have not played as well at regional as you did today because I don't think anybody in the state would have beat you today."

"The competition there was much better and we didn't play nearly as well as we did today, but at least we made it up here."

I could tell something was bothering Tommy and I thought I knew what it was.

"You miss coaching, don't you?" I could tell by the look in his eyes that he did.

"Yeah, I miss it. I should never have gotten out of coaching."

"Look, a lot of people talk to me about coaching jobs. I think I can help you get a pretty good job. Let me work on it after the state tournament is over."

The Pressing Champions

"Thanks, Johnny! I'd appreciate it. Good luck tomorrow. Given the way you played today, I don't think you need any luck."

I looked at him with a raised eyebrow. "You know better than that."

Leuders-Avoca, from the high plains just north of Abilene, was indeed a formidable opponent with an outstanding record. It was Friday morning and I was standing in front of my team before our semi-final game.

"You know, fellas, about twelve years ago I was in the fifth grade and I made my first trip up here to see this tournament. As a young grade school kid, I was totally mesmerized by the grandeur of this event. That lasting impression has remained in my mind to this very day.

It's one of the main reasons why I'm standing here in front of you right now as your coach. Although I was just a grade school kid, I knew I wanted to be a part of all this. That year, I watched a short, but very talented player from a small school not only lead the state in scoring, but also take his team to a state championship."

"Remember last year, we got Doc Hayes, the famed head basketball coach at SMU to speak at our athletic banquet? Well, that's where this player went on to play and play extremely well. His name is Max Williams.

"As a big SMU fan growing up, I watched him play many times for the Mustangs. I bet you're probably wondering why I'm telling you this. Any of you guys know where he played in high school?"

Coach Johnny Carter

When no one responded, I said, "He played for Avoca, the school you're about to play. In fact, he's probably out there watching this game today.

"Remember, we played these guys last year and they were the favorite. We upset them. This year, it's all reversed. We're the favorite and they have extra motivation to upset us, so let's go out there and show these guys that last year was not a fluke."

From the opening tip, we were in control with the full-court press paying big dividends and leading to several easy baskets. After leading 19–11 at the end of the first quarter and never trailing, we rolled to a convincing 82–66 semifinal victory.

Statistically, our shooting percentage was considerably better and we won the rebounding battle. Our hustling in-your-face pressure defense once again stood front and center forcing 20 turnovers and proved to be a major key in the game's outcome.

For the second straight day, we set a new scoring record for the state tournament. When you combine our score of 82 points today with the 92 yesterday, we broke the record for most team points for two games.

Just like yesterday, we had all five starters scoring in double figures. Again, Butch Walker was our leading scorer as he ripped the nets for 21 points, followed by Herman with 18, Roy 15, Haywood 14, and Nubbin 10.

James Creel was the leading scorer for the Raiders and for the game with 24 points. Larry Rister had a great

The Pressing Champions

game, ripping the nets for 18 and a game leading 14 rebounds. Bob Dody added 12. The disappointed look in their eyes and their grimaces said it all as we shook hands with this truly good team.

As we headed for the dressing room, Curtis came up to me. "Well, Coach, you've done it again. You made a good team look bad. After beating these guys two years in a row, I don't think they want any part of the Tigers."

I told Curtis, "You're right. They're a very good team, but we just flat out-played them today."

For the second straight day, I entered a joy-filled dressing room. There were a lot of smiles, but there was also a business-like look because we had just done exactly what we came here to do. We had systematically, through great effort, methodically taken down two very good teams with our intense pressure defense. The confidence factor in the mindset of our team was steadfast. Their faces were literally beaming and there was a glow in the room that personified it. This team fully expected to be playing for the state championship tomorrow and that's exactly what they'd be doing.

Gary Parrish came up to me with a big smile. "Two up, two down, and one to go. How about them Tigers, Coach?"

I smiled as Gary shook my hand.

"Everybody over here and have a seat. I think all of us probably thought that we'd be playing for the state championship tomorrow and now we are.

Congratulations on a great game today. It was a total team effort and we outplayed them in every statistic.

"Man, I'm proud of you guys. The last two days you have exemplified everything we've worked on all year long and the proof is in the outcome—two decisive victories. Tomorrow, you're going to be facing Friendswood, a highly disciplined team. They're much more conservative than we are, play excellent defense, and more than likely will try to keep the score much lower. Regardless, I think we're ready to play anybody and adjust whatever we have to do to win. Okay, let's get dressed and go get some lunch."

As we left the gym, I was walking with Richard Curry and James Smith. "Okay, you two are the only guys on our team that didn't make the trip up here last year. Tell me, how do you feel about this experience?"

Richard said, "Coach, this is an absolutely amazing experience. I've loved every second of it."

"How about you, James?"

"This is the most fun I've ever had in my life. I can't wait to come here again. Write it down, Coach. Before I get through with high school, we're coming back here."

As we left for lunch, I was smiling inside because the motivational factor was definitely entrenched in James's young mind. We were soon joined by James's good friend and fellow sophomore, Lester Hutcherson.

I couldn't help but continue to tease Lester about his phenomenal off-the-bench regional final performance against Frankston.

The Pressing Champions

"Say, Lester, I got a call from the letter jacket people wanting to know if that patch for your jacket should just say "Hero" or "Regional Finals Hero! What do you prefer?"

Lester rolled his eyes as he modestly tried to camouflage an almost hidden smile. "Aw, Coach, come on!"

James looked at me and said, "I think you should put big bold letters on the back of his jacket saying, "We're at state because of my man, Lester!"

Now we were all laughing.

Friendswood, our opponent for the state championship is located 20 miles south of Houston and 27 miles northwest of Galveston.

It was founded in 1895 when a colony of English Quakers moved to Texas from Kansas. After surviving the 1900 Galveston Hurricane, the Quaker influence remained in this community. The NASA Manned Spacecraft Center, located just ten miles from Friendswood, greatly influenced its growth in future years.

Chapter 16
State Final 1968

It was early Saturday morning, the day of the state championship game. We'd already had our pre-game breakfast and would be headed for Gregory Gym shortly. We had a short team meeting and I reminded everyone to be sure to check their travel bag to make sure everything that they needed for the game was in it.

"This is it, fellas, the last game of the year. I want you to go to your room. We'll be leaving in approximately two hours to go play the state championship game. Get off your feet, relax, and get your mindset headed in the right direction. I'll talk to you later."

Just as I got back to my room, the phone rang. It was my dad.

"I just wanted to let you know that your mom and I are praying for you, but that's nothing new. We've prayed for you every day since you were born. This has been a great season and I know in my heart that your team is much better than Friendswood, but you know as well as I do that the best team does not always win. I think you'll find a way to get the job done. This will be your toughest game of the three because of the style of play that they employ. You know that your mom and I love you and we just called to wish you good luck. See you at the game."

"Dad, Mom, thanks so much for always being there for me. I love you guys. See you after the game."

I believe that this special support and always knowing my family was there for me gave me that extra edge, not only as a coach, but in life.

Once at Gregory Gym, I told my guys to go to the dressing room and get dressed.

"We'll be warming up shortly, so don't waste any time."

A couple of minutes later, Gary Parrish rushed up to me with a worried look on his face. "Coach, I've got a problem! I screwed up big time!"

"Don't tell me you forgot your uniform."

"Not all of it, just part of it. I've got everything except my game pants."

"Well, son, do you think they'll let you play in a jock strap? That just might be interesting."

"Come on, Coach, this ain't funny!"

"Did you check your travel bag like I reminded you to do?"

"I thought I did."

"Thinking about doing something is not doing it. I'll tell you what, go out in the gym and find somebody that can go get your shorts. If you have to go with them, do it."

"Yes sir."

Coach Johnny Carter

In the dressing room, prior to the state final, I said, "Well, fellas, once again we've reached the mountaintop. It's been such a special journey and I've enjoyed every second of it. This team has achieved what we set out to do and I'm extremely proud of your accomplishments.

"You seniors, this is the last high school game that you will play in your life. I know that you're about to give it all you have. Make a special memory. This is your time, so make the most of it.

"You're about to play a team that will try hard to control the tempo of the game. They have an outstanding young coach, Walter Wilson. He has a young team. Their top four scorers are all underclassmen. Tom Long and Arthur Kahn are juniors. Don Reed is a sophomore and Kent Ballard is a freshman. They've played well in the state tournament, definitely have not played like underclassmen and they'll test you defensively.

"One thing that's beautiful about our style of play is that it's hard for other teams to totally control the tempo. That's what the pressing defense is all about. For the most part, it allows you to be in control. When you go out there this morning, I want you to have two things on your mind. Be patient, but at the same time, be relentless. Don't ever let up on the pressure because we can break a game wide open in a very short period of time. That's the beauty of our style of play. So, go out there and take it right to these guys! This is our time. Let's do it!"

One of the sweet sounds of the state basketball tournament was the mellow voice of Phil Ransopher, a long-time public-address announcer. After announcing our starters, he'd be in for a long day with four more state championship games to follow.

As I was going over our last-minute instructions in the huddle, there was that familiar voice in the background. "Ladies and gentlemen, it's time for the 1968 Class B state championship game."

The starting five for both teams walked toward the center circle and gazed into the eyes of their opponents, anxiously anticipating the uncertainty of the moment.

I then looked to the far end of the gym and to my surprise, I saw Gary running full speed in full uniform toward the bench.

"So, who saved you, Gary?"

"Mr. Van Dever got them for me."

"Well, you missed the warm-up, but at least you won't miss the game. You know a lot of people were looking forward to you playing the game in a jockstrap. In fact, the PA announcer already had his description of what to say if you scored."

Gary had an astonished look on his face. "You told the PA guy that I forgot my pants?"

"I didn't tell anyone, but everybody knows!"

Trying not to laugh, I said, "He told me when you scored he was going to say, 'Basket by Gary Parrish—that's two points for two cheeks!'"

"Thanks, Coach, you're all heart!"

With that, Richard Curry and Leeland Strban were about to fall off their seats laughing along with Gary.

Coach Johnny Carter

"Have a seat, son, we've got a lot of work to do."

Soon the ball was in the air as the opening tip signified the beginning this colossal clash. From the outset, the Friendswood Mustangs matched us basket for basket and had their game plan in full force. They basically controlled the tempo in the first half and went to the dressing room with a positive mindset.

The score had zigzagged back-and-forth until Nubbin hit a shot at the end of the first half to give us a two-point lead.

Walking into our dressing room, I knew I had to do something to get our mindset positive.

"Look, you have let a very young team THINK that they can play with us because basically that's what they've done. They're going to come out for the second half thinking they're going to control the tempo the rest of this game. This is the only way that they can play with us. The longer this goes on, the harder it's going to be for us to win this game."

I paused, looked around the room, and then with an emotional raised voice said, "The first half belonged to them, but I'm gonna tell you right now…THE SECOND HALF BELONGS TO US! You're going to go out there and from the outset take total control of this game. You've got to show them what kind of team we have.

"We have yet to do that in this game! You seniors, this is your last game. DIG A LITTLE BIT DEEPER! STEP UP THE PRESSURE! SHOW THEM WHAT IT'S LIKE TO

The Pressing Champions

FACE THE REAL TIGER PRESS! All it takes is a couple of steals to totally change the complexion of this game. All year long our aggressive defense has carried us. It has kept us in games when we didn't shoot the ball well. One of the reasons that I like the full-court press is that it can turn a game around, sometimes in an instant. You have got to put the fear of losing into their mindset because right now it's not there.

"That's the bad news, but here's the good news. You are about to put that fear into their heads and when you do this game will be ours. DO YOU HEAR ME?"

After an inspired, rousing response, my team headed back to the court focused on a very aggressive second half motivated mission.

We looked like an entirely different team at the beginning of the second half as our players seemed to take my halftime speech to heart. With fire in their eyes and a swarming full-court press, we started to really rattle the Mustangs. Nubbin stole the ball and then with a quick bounce pass hit Herman for an easy basket.

Immediately, our ferocious pressing defense caused another turnover, which led to a bucket by Haywood. All of a sudden, our stepped-up defense had Friendswood's young players on their heels. They could sense a major reversal in the atmosphere of this game-changing moment.

Sensing that the real Tiger team had just awakened from a deep sleep and was about to take control of this game, Coach Wilson had no other choice but to call a much-needed time out.

Our huddle was exploding with positivity as a fiery wave of enthusiasm had just catapulted us to a different level.

"I love free timeouts and your defense just gave us one! I told you the second half belongs to us! Now let's go out there and finish the job."

My guys couldn't wait to get back on the floor and when they did, they continued right where they left off. That positive frame of mind that the Mustangs enjoyed in the first half had totally disappeared as we continued to fan the flame. A hustling, determined, very aggressive team had just taken over this game and in a flash, had scored 10 unanswered points.

This Tiger turnaround totally ignited a spontaneous roaring reaction from our now standing delirious fans. They had observed runs like this many times over this season and fully expected this to be a part of today's game.

A jam-packed Gregory Gym had just witnessed the real Kennard Tiger team. In a little over three minutes, starting the second half our defense had virtually put this game out of reach. I had preached to our team all year about how explosive this pressing defense can be and how quickly the landscape of a game can be changed. Our relentless pressure had just put an exclamation point on this game and Friendswood never recovered. We went

The Pressing Champions

on to a convincing 64-49 victory and a remarkable second consecutive state championship.

Not quite as emotional as last year's after-game championship celebration, although a little more reserved, our fans were still ecstatic. We'd just achieved what all of our fans believed we would and, for that matter, what all the experts predicted would happen.

Now thinking and predicting are well and good, but what it boils down to is what you do on the floor when the chips are down and everything is on the line. We'd done that and then some.

From the outset, this team had been on a mission to defend last year's state championship and in so doing, they did it in style. We set a new state tournament team scoring record with each victory.

In scoring 92, 82, and 64 points in our three games, we set records for point production in a single game, two games and a three-game series. That total of 238 points substantially surpassed the old record established by Hutto High School's 218 points in 1964.

What a difference a year makes. Last year we weren't expected to make it out of regional and this year if we didn't win it all, it would have been a bad year.

Mom and Dad were first to offer congratulations. They were both thrilled, of course.

I was misty-eyed as I looked at my two very special parents.

"Thank you for everything you've done for me and your belief in me. I am so blessed to have the best parents in the world."

My two brothers were all smiles as they shook my hand. Billy said, "Well, Johnny, you won last year when you weren't supposed to and you won this year when you were supposed to—that's two great coaching jobs."

Then, with a sly smile, he said, "You keep this up and you just might make a pretty good BALL coach."

As we lined up to shake hands with the Friendswood team, there was a somber look of disappointment in their eyes. They weren't showing it at the moment, but deep inside there had to be a feeling of accomplishment because although they were a young team, they'd made it to the state finals.

Finally, I shook hands with Coach Wilson and we both congratulated each other on a great season.

"Walter, you did a great job with this young team. You've got them groomed to do something special next year. It wouldn't surprise me one bit if you guys are back up here next year with a different outcome. Congratulations!"

"Thanks, Johnny, I do appreciate it, but you're the one that needs to be congratulated. You've got one heckuva good team. That press totally took us out of the game at the beginning of the third-quarter. Up until that point, we felt real good about our chances."

"Thanks Coach. Good luck to you guys next year."

The Pressing Champions

"Speaking of next year, how about three in a row?"

With a quizzical look on my face, though hiding a slight smile, I looked back at Walter and said, "The good Lord has already blessed me with two miracles, three just might be too much to ask for."

On my way to the dressing room, I was again mobbed, congratulated, and hugged by our cheerleaders. Nelda looked at me and said, "It just doesn't get much better than this. It's been a great two years. Congratulations, Coach!"

"Thanks so much for being there for our team all year. You have no idea how much we appreciate what you cheerleaders do."

A smile appeared on her face. "It's amazing what you've done in your two years here! You have totally put our little town on the map!"

"Miss Nona walked up and gave me a hug, followed by handshakes from Curtis and Benford.

I turned to Miss Nona. "Okay, now for the most important question. Have I earned fried pies for the rest of the year?"

"I don't know about the rest of the year, but you'll definitely have one Monday morning!"

Everyone was laughing as I once again tried to head in the direction of the dressing room.

For the second straight year, I walked into the dressing room after winning that coveted state championship.

Coach Johnny Carter

From the first day of school to this magical moment, we could finally see all the glorious colors of that magnificent distant sunset emitting joyous rays of pleasure to everyone in the room. The atmosphere was glowing with handshakes, high-fives, congratulatory gestures, and all the hoopla synonymous with having reached the pinnacle of success.

That feeling of being on top of the world radiated on the young faces of every player on my team. I couldn't believe what we'd actually accomplished. Nubbin came up to me, shook my hand, and gave me a hug.

"It's all about D coach! You told me a long time ago that defense is the key to winning. Thank you for adding the pressing defense to our game. It made the difference today. It made the difference all year!"

Haywood added, "We wouldn't even be here if it weren't for that pressing defense. It carried us through the whole season. Thanks, Coach." With that, he gave me a big hug as well.

There were hugs all around. Herman said, "Thank you for coming to Kennard. We couldn't have done all this without you."

I was overwhelmed, almost to the point of tears with what was going on. It was such a humbling feeling, almost beyond description. I wish that every player and every coach that gave it their all could experience what we were experiencing.

It's called "winning" but actually what had just transpired goes way beyond that one word.

The Pressing Champions

Unfortunately, only one coach and one team in our class gets to experience this every year. I felt so blessed to be that coach at this time for this team.

I reached out and shook hands with Butch Walker. "Butch, you added so much to this team. I'm glad you joined us."

"Thanks, Coach. I'm just glad to be a part of this team."

"Let's hear it for our coach!" Gary Parrish shouted. Everyone was giving me an ovation as I wiped a few tears from my eyes.

"Thanks, fellas, now everyone take a seat. I want to thank every one of you for your contribution to guarantee the success of our team and I do mean everyone. I know some of you didn't get to play as much as others, but every one of you contributed. It takes that for any team to do well.

"Believe me, I've been a starter as well as a bench player, so I can identify with all of you. What we're experiencing right now is not totally about today and what just happened. It's all about the journey and the long road we traveled to get here. There were a lot of bridges that we had to cross to get to this point.

"You know the Green Bay Packers won the NFL championship this year over my Dallas Cowboys. Even though I pulled against his team, I have a lot of respect for Vince Lombardi, the head coach of the Packers. He once said something that's appropriate for you guys right now. *The man on top of the mountain didn't fall there.*

"Look, we have been climbing up that mountain from day one. There were a lot of obstacles, roadblocks, and hurdles that we had to get past to get where we are right now. These last three days are just icing on the cake. Think about all the practices, all of the ups and downs, adjusting to different situations and learning a new style of play. I am honored to have each and every one of you on this team. Thank you for listening and then applying what I tried to teach you. Thank you for believing in what I was trying to do. That's really what this is all about."

Roy spoke up. "We appreciate you thanking us, but what we really need to do is thank you. We've loved playing for you!"

With that, there was another rousing ovation and again I was moved to tears. What a special moment, what a special time, certainly one I have never forgotten.

As I wiped away tears, I looked into the eyes of this special group of young men.

"One more thing before we go. I really don't think you realize just how special this moment is. We've done something that many great teams could not accomplish. A lot of those teams trying to win a second consecutive state championship didn't even make it to regional, much less the state tournament. It almost happened to us. If it weren't for Lester coming off the bench in the regional championship game and making four of the biggest baskets in his life, we wouldn't be here now. Hey, let's hear it for Lester!"

With that there was a rousing ovation and Lester was all smiles. With an open hand and a congratulatory gesture to my sophomore bench player, I said, "Thank you, son."

"You six seniors who just finished your high school basketball career, savor this moment because you don't ever want to forget how you feel right now. Thank you, guys. You allowed me to live my dream, not once, but twice. Most people don't get to live their dream even once! It's been a pleasure working with you these last two years. You will be in my heart forever. Put this season in your memory bank because one day in the not-so-distant future, you'll be relaying this story and how this happened to your children, maybe even your grandchildren.

"I want you to promise me that when you say your prayers that you'll thank the Good Lord for allowing you to be a part of all this. You guys have already been in my prayers every day since I came to Kennard and I'll continue praying for you the rest of my life. I love you guys. Thanks again. Okay, enough said, let's go get some lunch."

Illustration by my son, John Carter

Chapter 17

An Earned Miracle

It was early Monday morning and I was enroute to school with about as good a feeling as one could have. For some reason, today's sunrise was more beautiful than ever.

I hadn't totally recovered from the intensive and hectic last two weeks which was a combination of the playoffs, the pressure, and finally the pleasure; however, there was a calm, relaxed feeling of fulfillment as I drove through the shadows of the Davy Crockett National Forest.

The serene, early morning sunrise peeking through the pines matched the feeling within my heart making this day even more beautiful. Approaching that last hill before reaching the school, I thanked the Lord one more time for allowing me to be a part of what had just happened. The vivid colors of this East Texas sunrise today seemed more spectacular than ever. Even the air seemed fresher as I walked from my car into the school.

I was met at the entrance by Emmit Roach, our principal. He reached out and shook my hand.

"Coach, you're two for two! I don't know how in the world you can top that!"

I just smiled and shrugged my shoulders. "You can't!"

"Congratulations, Coach, you have put this little town on the map!"

"It wasn't me, Mr. Roach, our team maybe."

"You did coach that team, didn't you?"

I smiled as I walked down the hall.

Before reaching the cafeteria, I ran into Mr. Van Dever, our superintendent. "Great year, Coach! It was an outstanding playoff run. Congratulations!"

"Thanks, I appreciate that. We reached our peak at just the right time."

I smiled at him. "I want to personally thank you again for rushing Gary to the hotel to retrieve his basketball pants. He was really shook up about it, but you saved him."

"Glad I could help out."

"I'm going to get a cup of coffee, would you like one?"

"No thanks, I've got a parent conference coming up. I've got to get right back to my office."

Coach Johnny Carter

The cafeteria was relatively empty when I walked in. With a cup of coffee in hand, I looked out the window, gazing at the breath-taking Monday morning. For most people, Monday is not the greatest of times because it's the beginning of the work week. That was not the case for me because I felt like I'd died and gone to basketball heaven. Having lived my dream for the second time in two years, I wondered what the future had in store for me.

Realistically, I knew that there was no way that I could continue at this pace. This was more fun than I'd ever had in my life and I knew I'd be facing an even bigger challenge next year. We'd be losing the majority of our team and would have a lot of unproven, inexperienced players. About that time a smile emerged on my face and I realized that I really needed to enjoy what had just happened this season and not worry so much about next year. As soon as that last game of the season is over, if not before, most coaches are thinking about what kind of team they'll put on the floor next year.

The door to the cafeteria swung open and a smiling Benford walked in.

"Well, Coach, you beat me here this morning. You look refreshed...like you must have had a pretty good weekend." He laughed as he shook my hand. "Do you know that you're totally responsible for my lesson plan this week?"

I looked at him, somewhat puzzled and said, "How's that?"

The Pressing Champions

"My shop class has to make another state tournament map of Texas for our gym wall."

"Great! It sure helped us out this year. We can put it right beside the other one. That will be double intimidation for our opponents."

"We do have one problem though."

"What's that?"

"You keep this up and we're not going to have enough wall space to put up another one."

I gave him a raised eyebrow look. "I don't think you have to worry about that."

We both were laughing, but then he replied, "I don't know about that, Coach. You have established a winning tradition around here and young kids emulate doing exactly what your teams have done. They're growing up thinking that they'll play for a state champion."

"I hadn't really thought about that."

With that, he looked me in the eye and said, "Hey, you've already got half the battle won. It's up to you to take them all the way. No pressure though!"

Now we were both laughing, but in my mind, what he said made a lot of sense.

Miss Nona came out of the kitchen with a hot apricot fried pie in one hand and the coffee pot in the other.

"Here's that fried pie I promised you."

I gave her a sly smile and said, "Okay, you told me after we beat Crockett in the finals of their tournament that I'd earned a whole bunch of fried pies. I think winning the state championship is just a little more significant."

We were both laughing now.

"Don't worry, Coach, you have many days of fried pies coming up and that's a promise. How about some more coffee?"

As she warmed up our coffee, she looked straight at me and said, "You've only coached two years and now you have two state championships. Hey, you're batting a thousand. Last year you were the youngest coach to win a state championship and now you've done it again. That's got to be some kind of a record. Congratulations!"

"I still have trouble believing all this. Sometimes I have to pinch myself to see if I'm dreaming."

"Okay, Coach, I've got a prediction for you. You're about to get a bunch of offers from other schools because you're one of the most desirable coaches in the state right now. You're not going to leave us, are you?"

What she said was something I hadn't even thought about.

"I have no desire to go anywhere else right now. I love my job here."

"You're going to be offered a lot more money to go somewhere else! Some schools will probably double what you make here, if not more!"

"If money was all I was interested in, I wouldn't be coaching...for sure not here. Money is not the number one priority for me."

The Pressing Champions

Although I wasn't setting the world on fire with the salary I was making, the rewards and relationship with the kids far outweighed the money.

Sir Winston Churchill once said, "We make a living by what we get; we make a life by what we give."

With a serious look on my face, I told Miss Nona, "I don't think my job here is anywhere close to being finished."

She walked back into the kitchen with a smile on her face.

Benford looked at me. "Coach, don't get me wrong because I don't want you to leave, but when you get those calls, at least check them out. Your career is just beginning. As time goes on, you'll probably go through a whole lot of interviews. Every time you go through one you'll learn something. It will be an invaluable experience for you and you never know what just might develop."

Later that afternoon I had my team sitting in the bleachers and I was having a talk to them about what had just transpired.

"I just wanted to congratulate you guys again on two incredible years. I hope that you did what I said and thanked the Good Lord for what just happened because you know without His help none of this would've happened. When you get right down to it, what we've accomplished is a miracle. You guys don't even know what it's like to lose a game of significance; in fact, as a coach neither do I.

"I don't think you can appreciate what we've done nearly as much as I can. You see, as a player I know what it's like to lose a big game and when it happens in your senior year, in many respects it's devastating. When Buna barely beat us in that heart-breaking regional championship game, some guy came up to me after the game. In trying to console me, he said, "50 years from now no one will know who won this game anyway!" I looked at him with a stone face and the competitive spirit came out in me when I said, 'I will!'

"This is one of the reasons why I pushed you guys so hard because I didn't want you to have to experience how devastating that can be, like it was to me. However, if you play long enough or, in my case, coach long enough, sooner or later you'll have one of those games and in many respects, it teaches you how to accept it. That's life!

"In so many ways sports are like real life. You don't always win! One of the main reasons I stand before you right now as a coach is that I have had trouble accepting this. Don't get me wrong. I can accept a loss, but it doesn't mean that I have to like it.

"I've learned through you guys to let a loss be a motivator. Two years in a row we lost a warm-up game and then came back stronger, hungrier, much better and won the state championship both years. You guys know what kind of a competitor I am and I'd like to think that some of that rubbed off on you. Apparently, it did because you've got two state championships under your belt. What we've accomplished in the last two years…believe me, it's not like real life! In some respects, we've been living in a fantasy world because what we've done the last two years is a true miracle.

"Here's what I'm leading up to. Yeah, it was a miracle, but it would never have happened had we not worked our butts off and you can mark that down! Look, we didn't just fall off the wagon, wake up one day and become state champions. It's all about hard work, team chemistry and total togetherness and you guys exemplified that! This was not your ordinary miracle, if there is such a thing. You check the practice time, the framework, the foundation, and what we went through, THIS TRULY WAS AN EARNED MIRACLE! Again, I congratulate you."

Later I called our four senior starters out of the gym and we went into a classroom.

"Look, I've got something that I'm very excited about to share with you. I know Cecil Ferguson, the new basketball coach at Angelina Junior College. I talked to him at the state tournament and he's very interested in all four of you guys playing on his basketball team next year. This is unprecedented for a Class B school to have all four senior starters be offered basketball scholarships."

Nubbin scratched his head and looked at me. "All of us, including me, Coach?"

Coach Johnny Carter

"That's right, all of you. He wants to offer all four of you guys a basketball scholarship. I'm thrilled. This has come about because you guys are winners. Every coach wants players on their team who have experienced great success and you guys have more than done that.

"How do you feel about playing basketball in college, Haywood?"

"Great! I can't wait!"

"How about you, Roy, how do you feel about it?"

"I look forward to meeting the coach. Yes, I'm very interested."

Herman then spoke up. "I can't believe that we can play together another year. This is great, Coach. I know you had something to do with this. Thank you."

"Actually, Coach Ferguson approached me with this idea. It was his idea from the start. I did give you guys a great recommendation, but he's the one offering you the scholarships. Now go home and share this with your parents and see how they feel about it. This is a chance for you to get your education started with a scholarship. Congratulations again."

Herman had invited me over for supper and I was sitting around the table with his family.

"Another great meal, Mrs. Myers. Thanks for inviting me."

"You're quite welcome, Coach."

Mr. Myers looked at me and with a contented smile said, "Congratulations on another great season, Coach.

The Pressing Champions

You guys just flat hustled your way to another state championship. When you can get guys to play that hard, great things happen. I've said it before and I'll say it again, I've never seen another team play with that kind of intensity, determination, and hustle in all my life."

"Thanks, Mr. Myers, I really appreciate that. I know they gave it all they had and that's really all you can ask from a team. And, speaking of our team, I need to thank you because this family, in particular, is one of the main reasons why our team has been so successful. You gave me Herman, our point guard, Nelda, our beautiful head cheerleader, Jeff, the point guard of the future, and I can't forget all of the wonderful meals that your wife prepared for me."

He had a pleased look on his face and Mrs. Myers was beaming.

Jeff looked at me. "Speaking of the future, I know it's a little early for me to be asking this, but what about next year, Coach?"

"We're going to be facing the same thing that we faced this year. Everyone's gonna be out to knock off the defending state champion. The bad thing is we're going to have to do it with a lot of inexperienced players.

"That doesn't mean it can't be done. You guys had a very good JV team, but there's a big difference when you go from JV to varsity. I think we'll be okay, but it's going to take a whole lotta work."

A few minutes later I found myself sitting across the table from Nelda as everyone else had left the table.

"Coach, it's been a great two years, pretty special. I really enjoyed cheering for you."

I smiled as I looked across the table at this beautiful young girl. "Well, the feeling is mutual because you did a great job cheering for us. In fact, you put all the other teams' cheerleaders in second place all year long."

Now she was blushing, but it was pretty obvious that she enjoyed the compliment.

"So, you're saying that you checked out all of the other teams' cheerleaders the whole season?" she asked.

"That's just part of the job. It's one of the fringe benefits of being the coach. You're supposed to check out and rate the cheerleaders."

"So, tell me, how did you coach and check out the cheerleaders at the same time?"

I gave her a sly smile. "It's basically a delicate balancing act. There's also a certain amount of skill involved and I think I'm pretty good at it. In fact, I must be *real* good at it because it didn't affect my coaching. After all, we did win the state championship...again!"

Now we were both laughing. I thanked her for the meal as I was leaving. When I got to the door, I stopped and turned around.

"By the way, using my year-long, sophisticated rating system, you easily came out an uncontested "number one."

Surprised and very pleased, she blushed. "Thanks, I really appreciate that!"

The Pressing Champions

Just as I opened the door, she said, Oh! I almost forgot! Don't leave yet. I've got something for you."

She rushed back into the kitchen and reappeared with a pie in her hands. With a smile and a look of accomplishment on her face, she handed me the pie.

"You asked me right before Christmas if I was ever going to make you a pie and since you did win the state championship again, it was time."

Smiling, I thanked her. "So, you're telling me that winning pays off!"

She thought about it for a second and then replied, "Yes!"

"I've got one question, would I be holding this pecan pie in my hands if we had lost?"

"Well, Coach, I guess I don't have to answer that question because we won!"

I smiled, thanked her again, and headed home.

Coach Johnny Carter

(L-R) Coach, Butch Walker, James Pilkington, Haywood Henderson, Herman Myers, Roy Harrison

Butch Walker:
All District, All Regional, All State Tournament;
James Pilkington: All District;
Haywood Henderson: All District, All Regional; All State; All State Tournament;
Herman Myers: All District, All State; All state; All state tournament;
Roy Harrison: All District, All State

The Pressing Champions

Butch Walker scores!
Notice map of state tournaments on gym wall made by Benford Frizzell's shop class.

All Regional Tournament Team

Regional Champions

Coach Johnny Carter

1968 State Champions

(L-R seated): Jeff Myers, Lester Hutcherson, James Smith, Richard Curry, Roy Harrison, Herman Myers, James Pilkington

(L-R standing): Clayton Baker, Walter Denman, Gary Parrish, Haywood Henderson, Leeland Strban, Eddie Ray Pilkington, Butch Walker, Coach Carter

Three state tournament scoring records:
  Most points in one game: 92
  Most points in two games: 174
  Most points in three games: 238

The Pressing Champions

Coach Carter holding 1968 trophy

1968 State Champions
(L-R) Roy Harrison, Leeland Strban, Herman Myers, James ('Nubbin') Pilkington, Haywood Henderson, Jeff Myers

Coach Johnny Carter

Roy Harrison

Butch Walker

The Pressing Champions

Herman Myers

Haywood Henderson

Coach Johnny Carter

James 'Nubbin' Pilkington

Gary Parrish

The Pressing Champions

1968 Cheerleaders
(L-R): Nelda Myers (Head cheerleader)
Carolyn Fowler, Mary Riley, Betty Hammond

Loyal fans John Dean Carter (standing),
Mary Frank Carter (seated, lower left)

Coach Johnny Carter

25-year State Tournament Reunion
for 1967 and 1968 State Champions
March 1992
Top (L-R) Coach Carter, Jerry Parrish, Fred Pilkington, Leeland Strban, Gary Parrish
Bottom (L-R) Herman Myers, Roy Harrison, James Smith, James Pilkington, Lester Hutcherson

The Pressing Champions

THE ROAD TO STATE IN '68

Kennard 79	New Summerfield 39
Kennard 67	Zavalla 30
Kennard 77	Richards 50
Kennard 77	Zavalla 35
Kennard 55	Woden 61
Kennard 74	Neches 60
Kennard 82	Maydelle 33
Kennard 78	Neches 69
Kennard 53	Big Sandy 49
Kennard 57	Hudson 35
Kennard 81	Central 52
Kennard 51	Central 47
Kennard 68	Buffalo 40
Kennard 62	Hearne 41
Kennard 61	Huntsville 38
Kennard 35	Snook 31
Kennard 72	Woden 50
Kennard 51	Hudson 43
Kennard 72	Brookeland 49
Kennard 88	Tomball 70
Kennard 74	Apple Springs 36
Kennard 72	Groveton 57
Kennard 58	Crockett 43
Kennard 66	Big Sandy 47
Kennard 68	Rusk 40
Kennard 81	North Zulch 50
Kennard 80	Rosebud 44
Kennard 59	Buffalo 39
Kennard 67	Tomball 35
Kennard 77	Centerville (Gr.) 51

Coach Johnny Carter

Kennard 86	Lovelady 48
Kennard 52	Apple Springs 36
Kennard 80	Groveton 55
Kennard 70	Redland 49
Kennard 74	Centerville (Gr.) 44
Kennard 78	Lovelady 34
Kennard 75	Apple Springs 55
Kennard 101	Redland 63
Kennard 52	Cayuga 54
Kennard 70	Central 48
Bi-District	
Kennard 91	Iola 52
Regional	
Kennard 67	Redwater 63
Kennard 64	Frankston 63
STATE TOURNAMENT	
Kennard 92	Prairie Valley 52
Kennard 82	Leuders Avoca 66
Kennard 64	Friendswood 49

STATE CHAMPIONS RECORD: 44-2

Chapter 18
Everyone Wants a Winning Team

The following week, Miss Nona's prognostication turned out to be right on. I had several schools calling, wanting me to interview for vacant coaching jobs. Amarillo High School flew me out there to interview for their head basketball coaching job.

Before getting off the plane, I made one last check in the restroom to make sure that I looked presentable. It was very windy that day as it quite often is in the Texas Panhandle. The wind did a number on my hair as I walked from the plane to the terminal. I looked like the wild man from Borneo.

I apologized to the school representative who met me at the airport for the way I looked. He laughed and said, "Everyone up here at one time or another has that wind-blown look, so you fit right in."

Nevertheless, I did make it through the interview and was offered their head coaching position. This would be a chance to go from one of the smallest schools in the state to one of the largest. I was flattered by their offer and although it was a much larger salary, much better working conditions, better facilities, and more prestige, I really didn't want to leave Kennard. I thanked them for their consideration but turned down the job.

Coach Johnny Carter

There were several other offers, one in particular came from Van High School. At Kennard, I became used to a shoestring budget, operating with just the barest of necessities. In fact, I used my own money many times when I was turned down on supplies that I thought we needed.

I was floored in the Van interview when I asked what kind of basketball budget I would have. The guy interviewing me smiled, took out a clean sheet of paper and laid it on the desk in front of me.

"Write down anything you want and you'll get it."

I was honored that people were pursuing me to be their coach, but the bottom line was I liked where I was and felt like there were still special things to come at Kennard High School.

It was early April in East Texas and as I sat in the cafeteria with Curtis, Miss Nona, and Benford, there was a lot of talk about the tragedy which occurred in Memphis, Tennessee. Martin Luther King had been assassinated. At this time, there was a lot of racial unrest in our country and this would trigger even more.

Miss Nona poured me a fresh cup of coffee. "There are a lot of misguided people in this country. Concerning the black-and-white issue, I know we're far from being perfect in our little school, but compared to most places, we're way ahead of the game."

Benford added, "It's all about respect, if people would just show respect toward each other a lot of this racial unrest would disappear."

The Pressing Champions

Curtis looked at me. "They just need to watch our basketball team and they'd see a perfect example of how blacks and whites can work together."

Before heading back toward the kitchen, Miss Nona looked back at me.

"I know you don't want to hear this again, Coach, but you and your basketball team have done more to bridge the gap between the blacks and whites in our community than you'll ever know."

"Thanks, Miss Nona. I do appreciate what you're saying. I just try to do my job, be myself, and treat every player as I would my own son."

There was a serious look on her face when she stopped, turned around, and said, "Well, Coach, just keep being yourself because we like what you're doing."

I looked at Benford. "Like you said, Benford, it's all about respect. When you respect each other that leads to unity and togetherness. I know that's one of the main reasons why our team has done so well. You guys know that I'm a fierce competitor and I hate losing with a passion, but when you have teammates that truly care for each other, it greatly lessens the pain of a loss."

"I know you know this, Coach, but you're going to be facing the greatest challenge of your young coaching career next season. You're basically going to have a whole new team and some of those same people who doubted you this year are already doubting you next year."

Coach Johnny Carter

Curtis added, "Yeah, they're saying that you were lucky the first year and you won the second year because all those guys were back. Now they say we'll see what kind of a coach you really are next year."

"So, basically what they're saying is if we don't win the state championship again next year that I've lost my touch."

"Coach, you've got the people around here spoiled," Curtis chuckled. "It's your fault, you shouldn't be such a good coach!"

"I know I have my work cut out for me. You just can't replace our four senior starters. It's definitely going to be a rebuilding year and I can't worry about what people say. To be honest, I'm not going to let it bother me one bit. Our JV team had a real good year and I'm hoping that they mature quickly because we'll be very young next year. If that's not enough pressure for the coming season, the UIL has reclassified us and moved us up from Class B to Class A."

I looked at Curtis and added, "You know something, I've always liked challenges. All I know is to work hard, give it all you have, and whatever happens happens."

As I headed for class, both Curtis and Benford were smiling.

Chapter 19
Tragedy

The rest of the school year just seemed to fly by. It was early May and one more school year was coming to a close. When I got to school that morning, I received some tragic news. One of my players, Eddie Ray Pilkington, had been killed in a traffic accident. Eddie would have been a senior next year and had his whole life ahead of him. He was the cousin of Fred and Nubbin.

Of course, the whole school was in shock. Everyone was in a state of depression. Eddie Ray was a handsome, very popular young man with a pleasant, happy-go-lucky personality. He would be sadly missed by everyone. It's particularly devastating in a small school. I was in shock as well because I was looking forward to working with him. Not having a Pilkington on our team for the first time was going to be hard to handle.

At the end of May was Graduation Day. Sitting in the audience, watching the ceremony, unforgettable nostalgic memories occupied my thoughts as I watched Haywood, Nubbin, Roy, and Herman walk across the stage. These four guys had been a major part of two championship seasons and they were absolutely irreplaceable. I was happy for them achieving a milestone in getting their diploma, but at the same time sad that they wouldn't be on the floor for me next year.

They were the backbone of our team and I hated to think about a season with them.

I congratulated them along with Leeland Strban and Walter Denman as we were graduating half of our team. "I'm going to miss you guys next year. It just won't be the same around here. Not many guys can say that they were state champions their last two years in high school. I congratulate you again. It's been a pleasure coaching you."

After a lot of handshakes, hugs, and sincere goodbyes, everyone went their separate ways. Driving home through the pines a myriad of memories totally engulfed my mind. *Was this the end of an era or could the young guys coming up keep the tradition moving forward?*

Chapter 20
Another Year

I had once again enrolled at Sam Houston State University to finish my Master's degree. Coming out of class one day, I was met in the hall by Aubrey Bradley, the superintendent of Chester High School. He congratulated me on our two state championships and then informed me that he was desperately seeking a basketball coach. "Do you know someone that you would recommend?"

I told him that I did have someone in mind. "Tommy Ferguson, a former classmate, teammate, and one of my best friends. He's a fierce competitor and I highly recommend him."

Tommy was working on a pipeline in Kentucky and when I informed him about the job he was elated. In fact, he put the phone down and started packing his bags immediately, drove all night, and knocked on my door in Madisonville the next morning.

"Johnny, you were serious when you told me you thought you could help me get a job. Thanks!"

"Glad to help you out, my friend. You were meant to be in coaching and this is a great opportunity for you. Look, Chester was in the regional tournament this year and they had some very good young players. You've got a chance to be pretty good." I grinned and added, "If you do some real BALL coaching, you just might be *real* good."

Tommy and I were both laughing and would spend many days during the summer discussing coaching techniques, in particular, full-court pressure defense.

The summer was coming to a close and I'd spent a lot of quality time with my family in Madisonville. I completed my Master's degree and at the end of the summer was headed to Dallas and the Texas High School Coaches Association Convention.

This was my second straight year to attend this and I was looking forward to not only a reunion with a lot of friends, but also some outstanding lectures from famous coaches. Tommy Ferguson and I were rooming together and after attending a lecture, we were on our way to lunch. Tommy and I had grown up big SMU fans and to our surprise on the other side of the street was none other than Hayden Fry, SMU's head football coach.

Without even thinking, Tommy yelled, "Hey, Coach Fry!"

To our stunning surprise, Coach Fry turned around, looked at Tommy and said, "How're you doing?" Even though he didn't know either of us from Adam, the famed SMU coach acted like he'd known us all his life. Tommy looked back at me with an "Eddie Haskell" grin as Coach Fry shook his hand and then mine. We would talk and laugh about this special day for many years to come.

The Pressing Champions

After attending coaching school, it was almost time to head back east for my third year at Kennard. My dad had given me a lot of advice in my life and he was very concerned about this coming season.

"This is going to be by far your biggest challenge in coaching. The experience factor is what I'm worried about the most because we're going to have a brand-new, extremely young team. In some respects, it's similar to two years ago when you took the job. However, two years ago nobody expected your team to do what it did. It's gonna be a little different this year because expectations will be high."

"I know, Dad, it's almost like starting all over, but you know I'm looking forward to it and I can't wait to get started."

As I looked into the faces of my brand-new team, I was just a little apprehensive about what was in store for me this year. Butch Walker was the only returning starter and Gary Parrish, last year's sixth man, were both seniors. Lester Hutcherson, James Smith, Jeff Myers, and Richard Curry were the only other returning members of last year's team. Obviously missing from this group was Eddie Ray Pilkington. I must say I had a heavy heart thinking about him not being there.

We had several newcomers, including Donald Denman, Larry Bruce, Johnny Burson, Jimmy Twine, Truman Lamb, Butch Jones, Frank Oswald, Carl Watson, and Roy Walker.

Coach Johnny Carter

"Fellas, you've got some awfully big shoes to fill. We'll be a totally different team than the last two years, but I promise you I'll give you all I've got and I'll work your butts off. If you're not ready to go all out on our full-court pressing defense, you might as well go home right now. I can promise you that the guys who do the best job on the press are going to be the guys who play the most. I expect you to give it all you have because if you don't, you won't be playing for me. Let's get that understood right from the start.

"Most of you will see significant varsity action for the first time. Let me tell you, this will be a major change. Going from JV to varsity is like night and day. You're going to make mistakes, but don't worry because I expect that. That's what I'm here for, to help you correct them. Don't be discouraged when I get on your butt for a mistake."

"That's my job as a coach. You have to look at a mistake as a learning experience, something that will help you in the long run. Look, I can overlook hustling mistakes, so make sure when you're playing that you're giving it all you've got. Anything less is totally unacceptable. Basketball should be fun, but it has to be played the right way. If you don't, you'll be sitting by me on the bench, if not up in the stands. We'll have a great year, I can promise you that and we'll have a lot of fun. Any questions? If not, let's get to work."

The Pressing Champions

While integration had been rather smooth in our little school, across the country it was pretty much just the opposite. Race riots, particularly in the larger cities, had become commonplace as evidenced in Watts, Newark, Detroit, and Harlem. Radical civil rights activists accepted violence as a means of protest, ignoring now deceased Dr. Martin Luther King's peaceful approach.

In the recently concluded Olympic games, Tommie Smith and John Carlos won the gold and bronze medals, respectively, in the 200-meter race. Standing at the podium, accepting their medals, they chose to wear a black glove, raising a fist in protest as the national anthem was being played. All this national racial unrest would be a major theme in the upcoming presidential election.

With all the racial problems across the country you would never know it at our school or with our team. The early season practices were going well. Our mindset was positive and even though we were making a lot of mistakes, we were definitely getting better. Our younger guys were really starting to step up in practice and this was encouraging because they were going to be a major addition for our team.

Lester was really looking good, evolving from the great regional final game that he had in Kilgore.

James Smith was going to give our opponents a lot of misery as the point man on our press, utilizing his great quickness. Jeff Myers, an ambidextrous sophomore, had the potential to become an excellent point guard. Don

Denman, another sophomore with great speed and quickness, would definitely see a lot of game time. When you combine these four guys, along with holdovers Butch Walker and Gary Parrish, we had the makings of a pretty good team.

The experience factor would definitely come into play this year because most of this team was young, having seen little, if any varsity action. The potential was there, but we were definitely a long way from what we'd done the last two years. Realistically, this is pretty much what I expected. A lot depended on how much improvement we showed once the season started.

During my off period, I was on the phone attempting to fill the last open date on our schedule. Finally, it was complete and as I left the office and walked down the hall, I saw Nelda coming toward me. This was my third year here. I'd watched this young girl grow up. She'd become more attractive every year. It was her senior year and she'd obviously had a good summer because she looked great.

"Coach, how was your summer?"

"It was good. I finished my Master's degree and to be honest, I was ready to start the new school year. I'm anxious to see what I can do with a brand-new team. You never know how a bunch of young guys will perform until they're put to the test."

"I'm sure you'll figure it out. My brother thinks that we're going to be pretty good."

The Pressing Champions

"Jeff is going to be a very good point guard. I hope he's right!"

As I headed toward the gym, I looked back and said, "By the way, you must have enjoyed your summer vacation because you look terrific...but I'm sure you hear that all the time."

"Thanks, Coach! I really do appreciate the compliment. It means a whole lot more when it comes from you." We were both smiling as I headed toward the gym.

Having won two consecutive state championships, it's assumed by some people that you must be cheating. I found this out one late September day when two coaches from Huntington, one of our new district rivals, showed up at our school.

I worked our team hard each day until the bell rang for school to be out. The rules stated that you couldn't start after school practice until October. We had open gym for anyone every day after school until about 5:00. As soon as the bell rang, I would go to the principal's office and work on lesson plans, write tests, or read the paper. I made it plain to those in the gym where I would be in case I was needed.

This particular day I was sitting in the principal's office when these guys showed up. They observed guys playing in the gym, then came down to the office. I was sitting there with a whistle around my neck, reading the paper. I honestly thought they were disappointed that they hadn't found me in the gym having illegal after school practice.

Nevertheless, I was surprised when I received a letter from the UIL a few days later concerning this matter. To put it mildly, I was not pleased! I immediately got on the phone, called Austin and explained what we were doing. The official I talked to said that what I was doing was perfectly legal and not to worry. He said he couldn't believe that he'd gotten a complaint about this in the first place. I always tried to stay within the rules and this incident reinforced that.

Later that week, I was discussing this matter with Curtis. He looked at me with fire in his eyes.

"Coach, are you as mad about this as I am? This really tees me off! If other coaches worked as hard as you do with their team, they wouldn't have time to mess with stuff like this. I guess they feel like if we got put on probation that their chances would improve."

"You know, Curtis, when this first happened, it made me as mad as a hornet, but I've gotten over it and I'm going to move on. A lot of different things motivate me to push my guys to be the best that they can be and guess what, they just hand-delivered a boatload of motivation to me on a silver platter."

Curtis smiled. "Coach, I don't know if you need any more motivation. You already have the most intense practices I've ever seen. So, I guess you're going to use this when you play those guys."

I smiled and headed for class.

Chapter 21
Inexperience

Our practices were definitely getting more intense because we were getting close to opening the season. One of the most difficult concepts to teach with the pressing defense is how to play with extreme intensity and not foul. When going one on one, it's hard to convince young players, in particular, not to reach while attempting a steal. When reaching, more times than not, your whole body moves toward the ballhandler, creating contact and a foul. We used what I called the "catch up" drill in teaching this.

By running tape along the length of the court and parallel to the sideline, we significantly reduced the boundaries for this drill. When I blow the whistle, a ballhandler and a defender standing on the baseline will take off toward the other end. It's the defender's job to cut off the ball handler and force him the other way, zigzagging the length of the floor. Emphasizing body position, proper footwork, and not reaching are constantly being stressed. When you combine that with the ballhandling skills required, it becomes a realistic facsimile of a game-like scenario.

Occasionally, you'll have a player with a sixth sense for stealing the ball. Coming up from the JV, James Smith was that kind of player. He had God-given extreme quickness and his reaction time was incredible. In order to utilize this uncanny skill, you have to give a guy like this more freedom and leeway than most players. With his incredibly quick hands, he would give our opponents a lot of misery as the point man on our full-court defense. I love the fact that the opposition had to get past him first to beat our press.

Coinciding with the beginning of our season was the 1968 presidential election. Earlier in the summer, Robert Kennedy was assassinated in Los Angeles where he was campaigning for the presidency. This tragedy occurred approximately four and a half years after his brother, President John Kennedy, was assassinated in Dallas.

With anticipation, I watched the election results with a good friend, Gary Cornelison, presently the coach at Slocum and a former teammate at Lon Morris Junior College. Playing for Coach Leon Black, Gary did something in practice one day that perturbed the coach.

Coach Black was irritated when he calmly looked at Gary and said, "Gary, Gary, Gary, the whole world is wrong and you're right."

I had to bite my lip to keep from laughing, as did everybody else on our team. Gary would exceedingly improve playing for Coach Black and become an excellent college player. Gary and I stayed up late watching the election returns.

Finally, there was a conclusion when the Republican nominee, former Vice President Richard Nixon, who lost the 1960 election to JFK, came back and defeated the

The Pressing Champions

Democratic nominee, incumbent Vice President Hubert Humphrey.

Before heading back to Crockett, I wished Gary good luck on the upcoming season. As a brand-new president was about to take over the White House, my team was also brand new. This totally occupied my mind on my long drive back home. We had several unproven, inexperienced, young players attempting the unenviable task of defending our two previous state championships. They would have to grow up in a hurry or it could be a very long year.

When we started the season, we actually played a little better than I anticipated. As expected, Butch Walker was our leading scorer, but we probably depended on him too much. As a returning starter and the only player with significant varsity experience, he also was our leading rebounder. Gary Parrish was also playing pretty well, but the most encouraging thing was how quickly our inexperienced young players were adapting to varsity competition. After Lester Hutcherson's incredible performance in the regional finals last year, it became pretty obvious that what he did was not just a flash in the pan. That became increasingly obvious with each of our early-season games as we started the season winning 10 of our first 12 games. Our full-court press was very effective early on with James Smith leading the charge. His speed and quickness, coupled with a great attitude, was daily inspiring our defense both physically and psychologically. In one of our early-season games, his value became even more evident.

Playing the front of our defense, pressuring the guy throwing the ball in, he unbelievably stole two consecutive inbound passes and scored both times in less than ten seconds. Now completely frustrated, the guy throwing the ball in totally lost his cool, reared back, and threw the ball at James.

To the shock and surprise of the guy throwing the ball in, James somehow incredibly managed to catch the ball deflected off of his chest, then scored again! Miraculously, in a little over 20 seconds, James had scored six unanswered points! The exasperated young man who threw the ball at James called timeout and took himself out of the game.

I had been preaching to my team that sometimes out of nowhere baskets can come in bunches and this legitimized my sermon. With each game, our young team was becoming more convinced that great defense was the key for our success. Perhaps the biggest surprise was the vast improvement of two of our up-and-coming sophomores. Jeff Myers and Donald Denman were adapting from the JV to the varsity extremely well. Both of these guys were smart and they caught on to the mental aspect of the game quickly. This allowed them to adapt to a much higher level of competition right away.

Two other sophomores, Carl Watson and Larry Bruce, also showed a lot of potential as did Butch Jones, a freshman.

The Pressing Champions

It was December 31, 1968, New Year's Eve. Tommy Ferguson and I were enroute to Houston to see the Bluebonnet Bowl, which was being held for the first time at the Astrodome. Tommy and I were thrilled that SMU, our favorite team, would be playing in this game against the University of Oklahoma.

We had a personal interest in this game after having visited with Coach Hayden Fry at coaching school last summer. SMU was led by All American Jerry LeVias, who helped break the color barrier in the previously segregated Southwest Conference.

It was an extremely cold night, much colder than normal for Houston and that howling norther had the wind chill factor much lower than the actual temperature. We were relieved that the game would be played indoors because it would've been miserable outside.

Hurrying from our car to get into the Dome, we failed to check exactly where we parked. We enjoyed a super competitive bowl game, and in the end, with the help of a touchdown by LeVias, SMU won 28-27.

We were excited about the game's outcome when we headed out into the cold. Thrilled that our team won, we didn't notice the temperature at first, but that changed in a hurry when we couldn't find where our car was parked. We'd exited the stadium at a different place than where we entered. That caused us to be totally disoriented. I think we walked around the dome a couple of times, but still could not find our car.

Coach Johnny Carter

We were literally about to freeze to death when I said, "To heck with this. I'm going to get a cab so at least we can search for our car out of the cold."

Getting into the cab and out of that bone-chilling freezing weather, Tommy was still shivering when he said, "You've made a lot of great decisions in winning those two state championships, but in my opinion, getting this cab just may be the best decision you've ever made!"

I wanted to laugh, but I couldn't even smile because my face hadn't thawed out yet. The cab circled the stadium three or four times before we finally spotted our car. The cab ride turned out to be money well spent. I think Tommy and I both learned our lesson with this experience. I still always check where I'm parked before leaving my car.

It was early January and the district race was fast approaching. Our record heading into the district schedule was 23–5. We had played much better than most of our fans thought we could. Our practices were getting more intense because I knew that the district race would be extremely competitive. Even though I wasn't a proponent of half-court zone defense, I had this idea of a special trapping zone. It looked like a basic 2-1-2 zone, however the man in the middle, James Smith, utilizing his superb quickness would be trapping the wings and corners on both sides of the court. James was one of the fastest guys I'd ever coached and I had no doubt about him being able to execute this. He was perfect for this role because he had the unique ability of being both quick and fast. James also had great stamina and never seemed to get tired. I was excited about this because it looked great in practice and would be a big surprise when we used it. I expected this to be very effective, especially against teams relying on a lot of outside shooting. After a strenuous practice, Jeff Myers invited me for supper.

Leaving the gym half an hour later, I drove the short distance to Ratcliff. We had a great meal and after everyone excused themselves, I found myself sitting at the table alone with Nelda. It seemed like this young lady got more beautiful every day. My mind was usually totally focused on basketball, but right now basketball was secondary.

When it was time to leave, she walked me to the door. "Do you think we're ready for the district schedule?"

"We're as ready as we'll ever be, but I'm concerned about how we'll react in this highly competitive race. We've got some real tough competition, but enough of this basketball talk. I just want to tell you that I've really enjoyed seeing you tonight. You helped me get my mind off what's coming up. By the way, you look beautiful.

If I thought I could get away with it, I would ask you out."

Coach Johnny Carter

Knowing I was joking, Nelda smiled and said, "Well, if you asked, I would go."

"You know, I've thought about this a lot and if we do go out, I'd probably get fired, but you know what, I think I'm willing to take that chance."

With a stunned look on her face, she said, "Are you serious? I thought you were just kidding around. You mean to tell me that you'd risk your job to take me out?"

"Why not?"

"I'm stunned! Just when are you planning on asking me out?"

I smiled. "How about the first Saturday in June?"

"That...that's not taking a chance! That's five months from now. I'll be graduated by then."

I laughed. "I know!"

We were both laughing as I stepped out onto the front porch. "Thanks for a great dinner. Be sure to thank your mom and dad for inviting me."

"I'll be sure to tell them. Oh, one more thing...first Saturday in June, eh? I'm going to hold you to that."

Chapter 22
The Challenging District Race

Our new district consisted of two zones. We were placed in the East zone, consisting of Huntington, Central, and Hudson — all straight basketball schools. Groveton was the only school in our zone that played football and they always had some good athletes. This had to be the toughest Class A basketball district in the state. The schools representing this district had won six state championships in the last 13 years. That's a lot of basketball tradition, so we definitely had our work cut out for us.

The district race was right around the corner and we had compiled a pretty good record leading up to the district schedule. As I had hoped, our defense was the backbone of our team and it was improving daily. It had basically carried us up to this point and how we performed in district play was contingent on our continuing defensive play.

I spent the weekend prior to the beginning of the district race in Madisonville, visiting with my parents. After church, we were sitting around the dinner table discussing the upcoming district games.

"Mom, that was a great meal. The roast beef was delicious."

Coach Johnny Carter

"Thanks Johnny, but hang on, I've made your dad's favorite…coconut cake."

My mom was a great cook and made incredibly delicious desserts. Today was no exception. After the meal, my dad looked at me. His expression was a serious when he said, "You've got some real tough games coming up. This is a tough district. Your team has done well up to now, but with all the inexperience that you're dealing with, it'll probably be considered an upset if you win this district."

"You're absolutely right, but my team doesn't look at it that way. In their minds, we're going to win it."

"Son, that's what coaching is all about, convincing your team to think positive."

"You know, a lot of people think that my team is a bunch of overachievers."

My dad smiled at me. "That's as good a compliment as a coach can have."

"Speaking of upsets and overachievers, the New York Jets are an 18-point underdog in today's NFL championship game. What do you think their chances are?"

"Not good, but you never know, that's why they play the game."

We turned the TV on and in awe watched Joe Namath lead his upstart Jets to an incredible 16 to 7 upset victory over the highly favored Baltimore Colts. Considered one of the greatest upsets in American sports history, this game was the first to officially bear the name "The Super Bowl."

The district race started the next week and I was expecting some extremely close, highly competitive games. We surprised a lot of people by winning our first three district games leading up to Central (Pollock), the team that I was most concerned about. They had made it to regional last year and had several excellent outside shooters returning.

Curtis had scouted them for me and when discussing our game plan, we agreed that our 2-1-2 trapping defense should be used. It worked very well, limiting their outside shooting as it minimized one of their strengths. When a good shooter hurries his shot because of a double team coming, it's usually not a high percentage shot. I kept a close eye on James Smith because he was all over the floor, but I never detected that he was tired. It turned out to be an extremely close game and the half-court trapping defense proved to be the difference, allowing us to win the game.

After the game, Coach Wyatt Dotson looked at me and said, "That was a heck of a defense you ran out there. You kept double teaming the guy with the ball and yet it looked like nobody else was open. We just didn't get many good shots. Man, your team hustles!"

I smiled and thanked him for the compliment. We went through the first half of district and finished in first place. I was elated with the success of our young players as they surprised a lot of people. Regardless of how we did the rest of the season, a message was being delivered for next year because most of our guys were first year varsity players.

Because of our youth, we were probably a year away anyway. Although we were playing well together and showed a lot of team unity, I felt that we weren't quite experienced enough to go too far. I never divulged this thought to our team because they were totally positive about us going a long way this year. When you get right down to it, that's a major part of the battle and that's exactly why I kept pushing them hard. A positive frame of mind can get you a lot of victories.

The second round of district was going exceptionally well. For a sophomore-laden team, we continued to astonish even our own fans by remaining undefeated in district leading up to our last game against Central. They were a seasoned team and as expected, Coach Dotson had his troops ready to play. The game went right down to the final seconds. We were one point ahead with two seconds left when one of their best players was fouled and would go to the free throw line. I told Jeff to call timeout right before the free-throw attempt. In fact, we called timeout again to try and ice the shooter. During the timeout, I told Jeff to discreetly tell the shooter before he got to the foul line not to blow this shot because it was the biggest free throw of his life. He badly missed the free-throw and we squeaked out a nail-biting victory.

The Pressing Champions

In fact, about a week later, we had a junior high game and, ironically, the same scenario developed. Just like before, I called two timeouts. This time the young shooter hit both free throws to win the game.

After the game, he came up to me and with a sly look on his face said, "Coach, I was at that game the other night. It don't work every time."

I looked him in the eye and as I shook his hand, I said, "Congratulations, son, you're pressure proof and you're going to be a very good player."

We ended up finishing first in our zone and would play Alto in a best two out of three for the district championship.

The city of Alto, as well as the entire East Texas area has a rich history of Indian culture. Over 1,200 years ago, just a few miles west of present day Alto, a group of Caddo Indians known as the "Hasinai" built a small village. Today at this site, three earthen Indian mounds still rise from the lush piney woods landscape.

The state of Texas actually got its name from the Caddo word "tejas" which means "friend."

Coach Johnny Carter

Illustration by my son, John Carter

The Pressing Champions

Chapter 23

A Heartbreaking Loss

Coach Pat Centilli's Alto Yellowjackets had a highly talented, well-coached team. Realistically, they were a much better team than we were. Although we had compiled a 31–5 record, it was going to take a superb effort, probably beyond our means, for us to stay with them. Basically labeled "overachievers" all year long, we had done this with great effort and a superb defense as we attempted to keep the tradition going.

Our close-knit team really thought that we were going to win this Alto series; however, led by Larry Jenkins, the talented Yellowjackets had too much manpower, defeating us in two games. It was heartbreaking for my young team and they took it hard.

When I got to the dressing room, I opened the door to see twelve guys weeping. It looked like a funeral parlor. I made a quick U-turn and went back outside, knowing if I went in there I'd be doing the same thing. I knew I had to go in, but before I did, I tried real hard to regain my composure.

I wasn't in there ten seconds before I had tears in my eyes. When you have players that take it that hard, it showed just how much passion these guys had for our team. It also says a lot about what is in the heart. Our team was hurting and the tears just kept flowing. As a coach, there's just so much you can say when something like this happens.

Having gone through this very thing as a player when I was in high school, I could definitely identify with them. It hurts more when you're a senior, so fortunately, this team was composed mostly of underclassmen. Hopefully this would lead to more determination next year.

Trying to be as upbeat as possible in a virtually impossible situation, I looked into the sad faces of my team and said, "Look at me. Get your heads up. First of all, I want you to know that I am extremely proud of each and every one of you. We had a great season, but sometimes things don't end the way we want them to. Life is full of ups and downs and that's what's so great about our sport. It teaches you to accept both the joy of a win and the sadness of a loss. Believe you me, you're going to face a lot of situations in the future that will make this seem rather trivial. We're going through a tough time right now, but you know what, tough times will pass, so let's get up and go home because we have many bigger bridges to cross down the road."

Years later, Robert H. Schuller would write a book entitled *Tough Times Never Last, But Tough People Do!* I knew that the young men I had on this team were tough and as these disappointed teammates finally started to exit the dressing room, I noticed that Lester lingered longer than anyone else. Finally, he was the last guy there.

The Pressing Champions

He still had tears in his eyes when he walked up to me and shook my hand.

"I want to apologize for not getting it done. Coach, I want to tell you something. I'll be spending the summer in Houston and playing a lot of basketball against those guys from Wheatley High School. When I come back next year, I promise you that I'm going to be a whole lot better. Coach, you can mark this down – we're not going to lose a game next year." He said that with a positive look in his eyes, then forced a smile and headed home.

Most coaches and fans look at a loss as a failure and when it happens during the playoffs, it's magnified even more. I tried hard not to look at this as a failure, but as a motivator. Robert Kiyosaki, author of the book *Rich Dad Poor Dad* which would become the number one personal finance book of all time, made a profound statement. Paraphrasing, he said, "Failure defeats losers, but inspires winners."

I hoped and prayed that this disappointing finish planted a seed and inspired that burning desire for a great season next year. As I drove back to Crockett, I already had next year on my mind.

Early the next morning, I sat in the cafeteria gazing out the window and wondering what I could've done to have changed the outcome of our last two games. My first cup of coffee didn't taste very good. It's strange how a loss can affect your taste buds, particularly a season-ending playoff loss.

Miss Nona came out of the kitchen and warmed up my coffee.

"Coach, this is the first time that you've experienced losing a big game. I'm not going to ask you how you feel because I think I know. I feel the same way."

Curtis and Benford joined in the discussion.

Curtis looked at me and said, "For all the youthful talent you had, this was a great year. I thought you got as much out of those kids as humanly possible."

"Thanks, Curtis. I really do appreciate that. They gave it all they had and realistically, that's all you can ask. I was proud of their effort. We just got beat by a better team."

With that older and wiser look on his face, Benford said, "Coach, you went 31-7. That's a heck of a record for a very young, inexperienced team. Most coaches would take that record in a heartbeat!"

I took a sip of coffee, then looked at him. "Yeah, but at this school you either win the state championship or it's a bad year!"

Benford chuckled. "Well, Coach, what you've done since you came here has totally changed how people think. Your teams have created an atmosphere of excellence. They expect championships. That's exactly why your team took it so hard and that's not a bad thing."

Curtis had a troubled look in his eyes. "I know you don't want to hear this, but I'm going to tell you anyway because I think you should know what's being said. Some of your critics are in that "I told you so mode" and they think that you've lost your touch."

"Hey, I expected that. It comes with the territory. It reminds me of a quote I once heard from John F. Kennedy. Paraphrasing, he said, 'Success has a thousand fathers while failure is an orphan.' Next time one of those guys runs us down, just ask him how many games he won last year."

When I was a player, I let losses linger way too long. In fact, that's one of the main reasons why I became a coach in the first place. As a coach, I was determined to move on as quickly as possible after a loss. An older coach once told me that players graduate and move on, coaches should always think about next year and move on.

My dad influenced me a lot in my life and one of the things that I learned from him was that there was always something positive out of every negative. He was a successful businessman, treated every customer with respect, and would always find something good in the worst of people. Dad applied the golden rule of "Do unto others as you would have them do unto you" every day of his life. His positive outlook on life greatly influenced me and right now I could see a lot of positives in our season.

Some of our fans didn't look at this year as a successful season. Well, they were dead wrong. We had most of our team coming back and they were just learning how to play this game. I really thought that our young team had learned a lot, maximized our potential, and I sincerely thought that we had sowed the seeds for a much better season next year.

Donald Denman hits a jumper

Lester Hutcherson scores again

The Pressing Champions

1969 Cheerleaders
L-R: Mary Riley, Barbara Davis, Jan Blair, Betty Hammond

1969 Team
Back row (L-R): Coach Carter, Clayton Baker, Richard Curry, Harold Walker, Butch Jones, Lester Hutcherson, Roy Walker, Don Denman, Johnny Burson, James Johnson.
Front row: (L-R) Jimmy Twine, Frank Oswald, Carl Watson, James Smith, Gary Parrish, Jeff Myers.

East Zone Champions
Record 31-7

Illustration by my son, John Carter

Chapter 24
Swarm of Bees

As I headed toward first period class, I was trying hard to put what just happened out of my mind. Believe me, this is easier said than done and even though I was working hard on it, so far it wasn't happening.

Before entering my science class, I ran into Nelda.

"Sorry about the loss. The guys are devastated and I know how it affects you."

"Thanks, I appreciate your thoughtfulness."

The Pressing Champions

As she headed for class, she turned around and whispered, "Three months and four days."

For a moment, I didn't know what she was talking about.

She smiled. "That's the first Saturday in June!"

I smiled as she walked away. Without even knowing it, she had taken my mind off of our loss and helped me move forward. All of a sudden, I had a much better feeling about teaching science this morning.

I was in for another surprise because after I took the roll for my class, Jan Blair, a very attractive brunette and one of our cheerleaders walked up to me. Although just a freshman, she had the look of a junior or senior.

"Coach, this is from our cheerleaders, we thought that this just might make you feel a little better." It was a nice card and at the bottom said, "We enjoyed cheering for your team. Thank you for a very good season. We love you." It was signed by Jan and our other cheerleaders: Betty Hammond, Mary Riley, and Barbara Davis.

I smiled and said, "Thanks, I really appreciate this. Please thank the other girls for me. I feel better already."

I had a team meeting later that day with all the guys who would be returning next year.

"I want to thank you for your concentration and effort this year. Despite what some people think, we had a real good year. You guys have learned a lot about what I expect from you and I think you gave it all you had.

Coach Johnny Carter

There's a lot more to a season than wins and losses. I couldn't be more proud of you. I love you guys. It's been a pleasure coaching you. I know that you're disappointed and so am I. At one time or another, I'm sure that each one of you have had some type of accident. You may have cut yourself and it bled for a while, but then the bleeding stopped and it healed. It may have left a scar. You look back on this and that scar will remind you of a bad time in the past; however, it should be like a bump in the road—you get past it and move on.

"Right now, this loss is simply a scar, but remember there's always a positive when you look at a negative and with me its motivation. I believe in this team and I can promise you that I'm motivated for next year already. Most of you are sophomores. I'm gonna tell you right now you didn't play like sophomores. When we went into district, you played like juniors! Sophomores don't do what we did in this tough district. Next year, I WANT ALL OF YOU TO PLAY LIKE SENIORS! It's going to require greater intensity, determination, commitment, and sacrifice. You do that and this team will turn some heads. Next year I want us to step up our game to a much higher level and when you do, we're not gonna have just a good season, WE'RE GONNA HAVE AN EXTRA SPECIAL SEASON!

"Lester, next year will be your senior season. You want to have an extra special season, don't you?"

"Coach, we're going to have a great season! I can feel it in my bones."

The Pressing Champions

The bell ending the school day had just sounded. I was about to go home early, something I hadn't done all year. For the first time in my brief coaching career, my team wasn't practicing for a playoff run.

As I walked toward my car, Bob Currie got out of his truck and stopped me.

"Coach, I wanted to tell you how much I appreciate what you've done in the short time you've been here. I just happened to walk by the dressing room after the game. I see now why your teams have done so well. When your players show that kind of emotion after a setback, it not only shows their passion for our team, but how they feel about their coach. They didn't want to let you down."

"Thanks, Bob. I wish more people could see the big picture as well as you have."

"Coach, you probably won't agree with what I'm going to say, but in my opinion this year was your best coaching job."

"Thanks, Bob. I needed to hear that."

"From the first game to right now, this team improved a ton. It really makes me look forward to next year. If you can get this team to improve that much next year…look out!"

I looked at Bob and smiled. "I'm also looking forward to next year."

It was good to know that a school board member and one of the most influential men in our community felt this strongly about what I was doing.

Coach Johnny Carter

After the last two years, it felt kind of strange going to the state tournament strictly as a fan. I was sitting in the stands with two of my best friends, Tommy Ferguson and John McGilvra. I had previously helped Tommy get the head coaching job at Chester High School and John was the new coach at Diboll. We were talking about next year and the fact that each of us felt like our teams might have playoff potential.

Tommy was usually joking around, but he made a serious statement.

"Wouldn't it be great if all three of us brought our teams up here next year?"

John laughed and said, "I can see Carter coming up here again, but for you and me, it'll probably take a miracle!"

We all laughed, but a serious thought occurred to me. "Anytime your team is fortunate enough to get up here, it's a miracle!"

Tommy looked at John and smirked. "We'll find out real early just how good we are next year because both of us have got to play Kennard twice."

John said, "Yeah! Like I'm really looking forward to facing that Kennard press. You are going to press, aren't you, Carter?"

With a slight smile I said, "Not until you get off the bus!"

Now we were all laughing. It was fun seeing my good friends and reminiscing. There were a lot of coaching

The Pressing Champions

stories being exchanged and we truly enjoyed the tournament.

I had a particular interest in two of the teams in the finals that we had played in the past. We had beaten Snook in the finals of the Madisonville tournament last year, but this year they came right back to Austin and won the Class B state championship for the third time.

Although no surprise to me and just as I had predicted, Friendswood was once again in the state finals. We had beaten them in the state championship game last year, but this year they refused to be denied again and won the Class A state championship 51- 49 over West Sabine.

Later that spring after track season was over, we were working during the athletic period for next year. For the most part, our season had been defined by our pressing defense. I was determined to refine it and make it much more effective. I wanted every player on our team to look at each defensive opportunity as a time in which we were in total control. Having a positive mindset whenever we were pressing was something that I constantly stressed. When that situation arrived, no telling how many times my team heard me say, "We got them right where we want them."

That day during practice, I noticed a slight let up in effort. Perturbed by what I saw, I quickly blew my whistle and everybody froze. "That is not acceptable! There are some mistakes that are unavoidable and believe me, I totally understand that. I don't worry about those types of mistakes; however, I will NEVER accept even the slightest lack of hustle. So, when you do make a mistake, you better be busting your butt. If you don't give it all you have, particularly when we're running our pressing defense YOU WON'T BE PLAYING FOR ME!

"I want you to be so aggressive that you create an illusion that makes all of our opponents think that there's a SWARM OF BEES ATTACKING THEM! Make it look like we have six or seven guys going against them! You need to instill fear in them, create a mindset of constant frustration. When you deny passing lanes, guess what? You create chaos. This only happens when everyone does their job and works together in a unified effort, just like the worker bees.

"Let me make this perfectly clear. YOU WILL DO THIS! Look, there's going to be times when you're dead tired and think you can't take one more step. Listen to me! That's when you dig a little bit deeper. You'll be surprised what you have left in the tank when you're determined to get the job done. Let me make this perfectly clear because I don't ever want to have to repeat what I just said!

"Don't ever squander a defensive opportunity! Every time we play defense, that's our time. WE OWN THAT TIME! If you let up just one time, that's like giving up and it can cost you a game."

"So, what am I saying here?"

The Pressing Champions

Donald Denman looked at me and said, "If you never let up, you won't give up."

"That's exactly what I'm saying. Don't ever let up. There are many ways to lose a game, most of which as a team we are totally in control of. As your coach, it's my job to show you how to eliminate as many of those controllable reasons for losing as possible. Mark this down. WE WILL NEVER LOSE A GAME BECAUSE OF A LACK OF EFFORT!"

Galatians 6:9 says, "Let's not get tired of doing what is good, for at the right time we will reap a harvest – if we do not give up."

After this practice, our team showed remarkable improvement in the intensity of our press defense. I always thought the key to teaching this was repetition. I wanted our guys to know the fundamentals of our defense backwards, forwards, and sideways. When a team consistently gives great effort over and over, the chance for success will always be there.

Coach Johnny Carter

As the school year came to a close, our defensive execution was really starting to come around. I always looked forward to the summer vacation, but with the work ethic that my team was showing right now, I wanted to keep right on practicing. We were much farther along for a young team than I ever anticipated and I was really fired up about next year.

Chapter 25
First Saturday in June

Nelda Myers

It was graduation day and after shaking hands with Butch Walker and Gary Parrish, I wished them well. "It's been fun working with you guys. I had hoped that our team would go a little farther, but you know what, we had a good year. I'm proud of you guys." I would miss these two left-handers next year.

Nelda walked up to me. She was wearing a beautiful dress and a smile to match.

"Well, Coach, I finally graduated."

"You know, this is the third graduation ceremony that I've been to since I came here. This is by far and away the best graduating class."

"Why is this class so special?"

I smiled at her and said, "Because you're in it, that's why."

She smiled, then said, "You're coming to my graduation dinner, aren't you?"

"Yeah, your mom already invited me. I'll be over there shortly."

I'd enjoyed many meals at the Myers' home over the last three years, but for some reason, tonight's meal had a much bigger meaning. It was another wonderful meal. As usual, after dinner I was again sitting at the table, alone with Nelda.

"You know, you came to that graduation ceremony as a very attractive young high school girl and you stepped off of that stage as a beautiful young lady."

Nelda blushed as I continued.

"It's amazing what getting that diploma in your hands does. One day you're frustrated because you're on the bench unable to get into the game, then all of a sudden, the next day you move up to a starting position and become a highly sought-after player in a totally different game. Congratulations, you're now in the real game and I'm looking forward to being your personal coach."

Nelda was blushing as she took in all of these compliments. "Keep talking, I like what you're saying."

"First of all, you don't have to call me 'Coach' anymore. Second, you looked real nice in your cap and gown, but you look great in that dress. Third, tomorrow is the first Saturday in June."

The Pressing Champions

She laughed. "I was going to remind you about tomorrow, but you beat me to the punch."

"I'm really looking forward to tomorrow night. It seems like it took forever to get you graduated."

"Tell me about it. Believe me, I know. That's past history now and like you said, I'm now in the game."

"Do you mind if I change clothes? This dress is just a little too formal for me."

"Before you do, I just want you to know how stunning you look in it."

"Thank you. I really appreciate that. I'll be back shortly, make yourself comfortable."

Actually, the graduation outfit was perfect for her, but when she came back in the room wearing those short shorts, I totally forgot how that dress looked.

"Wow! I didn't think you could top how you looked in that dress, but I stand corrected. I definitely approve."

"Thanks, Coach...I mean Johnny. It's going to be hard for me not to call you Coach."

"That's okay. Look, I know it's not Saturday yet, but how do you feel about getting off to an early start? Come on, let's go for a ride."

As we walked outside, I suddenly stopped in my tracks and looked at her. "Can you believe that this day is finally here?"

"No, but I'm sure glad that it is."

"I hope you're not disappointed."

"Believe me, Coach...I'm sorry! I mean Johnny."

"Hey, don't worry about it, everybody calls me Coach."

"I can see I'm going to have to work really hard at not calling you Coach. Let me try this again. Believe me, JOHNNY, there's no way that I will be disappointed. I've looked forward to this night for almost two years. I just hope that you're not going to be disappointed."

"Look, I've had my eye on you for a long time, patiently waiting for this night. Now that it's finally here, let's forget about this disappointment talk and just have a good time."

I opened my car door for her, but before she got in, I said, "I've often wondered what it would be like to kiss you. I'm tired of waiting."

With that, I looked in her eyes, held her face gently with my fingertips, and kissed her ever so softly.

She got into the car, then looked at me and asked, "Was it worth the wait?"

"Oh yeah...and I am definitely NOT disappointed!"

We drove around for a while, just enjoying each other's company. Ironically, on Nelda's graduation night, the song on the radio was Simon and Garfunkel's "Mrs. Robinson," the theme song from the movie "The Graduate."

Later, we went for a walk at Ratcliff Lake. It was a very still, early summer night in East Texas. The back drop of pine trees and the reflection of a full moon off the water made this one beautiful night, especially when accompanied by a very attractive young lady. At this very special moment basketball was the furthest thing from my mind.

We had a wonderful time and it was a great first date. I walked her to the door, held her in my arms and gave her a long goodnight kiss.

She looked at me, smiled, and said, "I had a great time. Thank you."

"It was fun. We'll have to do this again real soon, like tomorrow night; however, I've got to confess, I am disappointed."

A stunned look appeared on her face. Unable to keep a straight face any longer, I smiled and said, "I am disappointed...that this evening is over."

With that, we both laughed and I headed home. I think that was the first time that I made that drive through the pines thinking about something besides basketball. All of a sudden, the sadness and disappointment in the way our season ended just didn't seem all that important. Nelda and I would see each other quite often in the coming months.

A few weeks later, it was the middle of the summer—July 20, 1969. I was glued to the television along with a half-billion others watching Apollo 11's moon landing. History was made at 9:56 CDT when astronaut Neil Armstrong became the first man to set foot on the moon. After accomplishing this remarkable feat, he made the unforgettable statement, "That's one small step for man, one giant leap for mankind."

Coach Johnny Carter

Mesmerized by what had just happened, I walked outside and gazed into the heavens. I stood there for a long time, staring at the moon, completely captivated. It was mind-boggling to me looking at it, knowing there was actually a man walking on the moon's surface. This spectacular event made winning two back-to-back state championships seem rather trivial.

As most summers go, this one flew by and it was time to start school for my fourth year at Kennard High School. Even though I loved the summer vacation, the way my team had been practicing at the end of school had me raring to go and get back in the gym. I must say that I missed not seeing Nelda walking down the hall, but she was now in college.

I did see a couple of guys coming toward me that I was glad to see. Lester Hutchison and James Smith, the only two seniors on this year's team came up to me. Lester looked at me and said, "Well Coach, how was your summer?"

"Great. How was yours?"

"I played a lot of basketball in Houston and I can't wait to start this year. We've got some unfinished business to take care of."

James joined the conversation "I thought about the way our season ended all summer. I don't think I'll ever get over it."

"Just be thankful that you two guys have one more year. Think about how you'd be feeling if you'd finished school last year. How do y'all feel about this year?"

The Pressing Champions

James quickly responded, "Coach, our press was pretty good last year. This year I want it to be *real* good."

I smiled. "Let me put it to you guys this way, if you want to have a great year, then we have got to have a great press."

James smiled, looked at Lester and then back at me. "Then we'll have a great press!"

I looked at these two young men. "Great pressure defense can be the absolute answer for our lack of size."

As they headed for class, I thought to myself just how blessed I was to have these two young men as the leaders of my team. Not only were they good players, they were good guys and they had great attitudes. They were determined, focused, very coachable, and would do whatever it took to make our team successful.

Chapter 26
You Did Not Run Back HARD!

Our early season practices were very encouraging. I was expecting big things from Lester and James. Our team needed major contributions from these two guys and I felt like we would get that.

Jeff Myers and Donald Denman had impressive sophomore seasons and both were already showing improvement from last year. The fifth starter position was up for grabs, but in our early practices, Carl Watson, another junior, appeared to have a slight edge. Larry Bruce and Butch Jones, a junior and a sophomore, respectively, were definitely right there as well. Defense had always been first and foremost in our practices and I planned on it being that way again this year.

For the most part, my players had seen the impact of our full-court pressure defense for the past two years. I counted on the carryover tradition of the past to significantly influence the future. When you have four starters returning, it greatly enhances that possibility.

Two years ago, we had four starters back and won the state championship; however, they were returning from a previous championship team. This year we were returning four starters coming back from a 31-7 team that was knocked out early in the playoffs. I hoped that

The Pressing Champions

the way our season ended last year would trigger a burning desire to go much farther this year.

In our first month of practice, I could definitely sense that to be the case because this team was hungry for a bigger and better season. Daily, there was an increasing determination to disprove the downcast dismal ending of last year's early playoff exit. When you have a team with that mindset, it makes walking into the gym each day a sheer pleasure.

It was early October 1969. The seasonal landscape was changing as the leaves on the deciduous trees were starting to fall. So far, this had been a year of upsets and firsts with the Jets winning the Super Bowl and the first man to walk on the moon.

The year was not yet over and another amazing event in the sports world was about to happen. The New York Mets, for years the laughing stock of major league baseball, were about to pull off perhaps the biggest upset in the history of the World Series. In the previous seven years of their existence, this expansion team had never finished higher than ninth place in a ten-team league. Led by future Hall of Famer's Tom Seaver and a young Nolan Ryan, they became the "Miracle Mets" when they defeated the Baltimore Orioles.

My dad and I loved to watch baseball games together and we thoroughly enjoyed seeing the underdog rise to the top. We had witnessed this firsthand with our first state championship as we were the underdog in every playoff game.

Coach Johnny Carter

In preparation with the short time remaining until our first game, our intense pre-season practices were getting longer and longer. Meanwhile, the fashion industry was continuing to dictate that women's skirts were going to be shorter and shorter. Miniskirts had become commonplace and were very popular, particularly with the guys. One girl in our school was the absolute trendsetter in this area. Jan Blair, an attractive, leggy brunette was constantly wearing very short skirts. She set the fashion trend at our school as the skirts went from mini to micro-mini!

Jan had been elected head cheerleader and although just a sophomore, she had the look of a senior. She took that role seriously and in a meeting with me, wanted to know what I expected from the cheerleaders.

"If there's anything you want us to do besides cheering at games, just let me know. I think our main job is to do everything we can to help make your season successful."

"Thanks for asking, Jan. I appreciate your attitude. Actually, one of the main things you can do is to encourage the guys when you see them in the hall. Tell them that they played a great game. It's amazing what singling out a player off the court does for their productivity on the court. When you tell a player that you really enjoy cheering for him, it makes that guy feel very important and greatly enhances the way he plays. I'm constantly correcting players in practice, but I try real hard to do it from a positive perspective. In some respects, as the head cheerleader, you'll probably be doing the same thing."

"Thanks, Coach. I will definitely get this point across to our other cheerleaders and if there's anything else during the course of the season that you want us to do, just let me know. I want to do everything that we can to ensure that you have a chance for a perfect season."

I looked at her and smiled. "It's virtually impossible to be perfect, but it's something that you strive for every year. By the way, you look more like a cheerleader in that short skirt than those outdated cheerleader outfits y'all had last year. I hope you girls get some new uniforms."

"Thanks for the compliment. Yes, we're going to get some new cheerleader uniforms. Bob Currie's wife, Margie, has made us some brand-new outfits and they look great. I think you'll like them."

She got up to leave, then stopped and turned around. "I almost forgot! This is for you." She opened the package she had brought in and handed me a cake.

"This is a bundt cake that I baked especially for you."

"Well, thank you very much. I appreciate that."

With just a few days of practice remaining until our opening game of the season, our preparation was getting more serious. Outside it was getting colder as the first norther of the season arrived, signifying the coming of winter. That howling sound was playing a tune as it whistled through the pine needles.

Coach Johnny Carter

In the warmth of our little gym, we were having an intense workout, implementing our full-court press defense. Larry Bruce got through our press, creating a three-on-one and made a quick pass to Lester Woods who, in turn, hit George Steed for an easy basket. Seeing that we didn't run back down the floor as quickly as possible, I blew my whistle.

Even though it was getting colder outside, I was hot! With a raised voice of disapproval, I forcefully said, "First of all, they went through your press like grass through a goose! Second, when you run back down the floor with a piano on your back, a lot of ordinary teams are going to kick your butt. We have one guy back there guarding the basket and he can't do the job by himself. Any time they get through our press like that, I'd better see all-out sprints back to the basket to help him out.

"Look, you guys thought you ran back, but listen to me. YOU DID NOT RUN BACK HARD! When it comes time to run, I expect you to RUN!" The word run was now echoing off the walls of our little gym.

"Do you understand?"

There was a faint, almost apologetic "yes sir" in the background. "I can't hear you!" There was a much louder response after that.

"Look! Do you want to go in the dressing room after a loss and have to look me in the face when I say to you, 'We lost that game because YOU didn't run back hard?'

The Pressing Champions

"If you want somebody else doing your job, then keep running back down the floor like that and there'll be somebody else out there in your place.

"Look, I don't think any of you guys are lazy, but the way you ran back down the floor that time YOU LOOKED LAZY! "When applied to basketball, Proverbs 13:4 addresses this. 'Lazy people want much, but get little, but those who work hard will prosper.' "Listen to what I'm about to say and get it magnified in your mind!

"WE WILL NOT GIVE UP EASY BASKETS! This is what I expect and it better be what I see out there on that court! If we're going to run the full-court press, we're going to execute it my way! Is that clear, sports fans? Okay, let's give it another shot and see if we can do it right."

I think my point was well taken because later on in the practice we had a similar scenario, only this time it looked like four guys were shot out of a cannon because there was an all-out sprint to get back to the basket.

"Now that's what I'm talking about! You got back into the paint in a hurry and PREVENTED an easy basket."

As a student of health, I have always been a proponent of prevention being the best cure. That's certainly the case when considering this aspect of our defense. Many coaches abandon this style of game because getting back down the floor is just not stressed enough. It's hard to convince players to sprint back down the floor when they're dead tired, but it can be done. This is what I call "basic bottom line bust your butt, blue-collar, fundamental basketball."

It's probably the most important objective that has to be implemented with full-court pressure defense. This is not as glamorous as making a steal, scoring a quick basket, and totally turning a game around, but I'm telling you right now, it's just as important. Besides, you'll be surprised at how many turnovers and steals are created by racing back down the floor like the Pony Express. Obviously, the main objective here is to be in great shape because while consistently sprinting back down the floor greatly enhances the proficiency of the last line of defense, it definitely will test your endurance.

I walked through the dressing room and all the players, with the exception of Donald Denman and Jeff Myers, had already left. Not only were these two guys becoming very good players, they were both highly intelligent.

Jeff said to me, "Coach, I don't think any of us realized that we weren't getting back down the floor hard."

Donald looked out of the corner of his eye at me. "I didn't realize at that time that I wasn't going full speed." His expression was apologetic, then changed to a sly smile when he said, "But I dang sure do now!"

Looking at Donald, I said, "Well you better! You're one of the fastest players on our team and if you don't utilize it fully, we're never gonna realize just how good you can be."

The Pressing Champions

"It won't happen again, Coach, and that's a promise."

"I know it won't, son, because I think you'd rather be out there on that floor than sitting beside me on the bench...RIGHT?"

Shaking his head in a positive manner, while attempting to camouflage a smile, Donald replied, "Right."

"Jeff, you're my point guard, right?"

"Yes sir."

"I expect you to be my assistant coach on the floor. You see something out there that's not right, I expect you to fix it. Saving me a timeout is valuable. Having extra "time outs" in the last couple of minutes can give us a chance to win a game that we would normally lose. Can you handle that?"

"Yes sir."

"Good, because I'm gonna hold you to that."

Chapter 27
Total Team Togetherness

Our season was about to begin and I must admit that I was a little bit apprehensive about how it would play out. When I came here three years ago, the players on our team now were in the ninth grade or in junior high. This would truly be the first team that had totally grown up under my system. I had coached these young men from day one and I was anxious to see how they would respond as the backbone of our team.

This team was very young last year and although one year older, they were still young because a majority of the players were juniors. I was sitting in the cafeteria having a cup of coffee with Curtis and Benford.

Curtis looked at me and said, "Well, Coach, are you ready for tonight's opening game?"

"I'm always ready. I just hope my team is."

Benford smiled. "I just talked to Lester and he's raring to go."

"You know, two years ago when he came off the bench in the regional finals and pretty much won the game for us, I knew that he was going to be a very good varsity player. To be as thin as he is, he just gets the job done. He has a lot of basketball savvy."

Benford said, "We expected Lester to be good, but has anybody surprised you so far?"

The Pressing Champions

"The biggest surprise has been Carl Watson. He has really impressed me in practice and is going to be a major contributor."

Curtis looked up from his coffee cup. "Your first two games are with Apple Springs, our old district rival. It should be interesting. Well, Coach, all of the Monday morning quarterbacks and doubting Thomases are coming out of the woodwork again. One guy yesterday that always seems to question how you're going to do said 'we'll all find out just what kind of a coach Carter is this year because the talent is just not there.' He doesn't think we'll do any better this year than we did last year."

I smiled. "I expect criticism, that's just part of the job. It's true that our talent is not what it was with our two previous state championship teams, so we're just going to have to be more efficient. Our key is going to be teamwork and if we don't get that in a big way, this team could be ordinary. Believe me, this is constantly being stressed every day in practice. We have to be unified with togetherness in every aspect of our game.

Coach Johnny Carter

Illustration by my son, John Carter

In a way, I like to compare our team to the giant redwood forest along the Pacific coast. These are the tallest trees on Earth, soaring well over 300 feet and about 100 feet taller than our tallest pine trees."

Benford looked at me and laughed. "Come on, Coach! Are you trying to tell me that you're going to compare our little guys to those huge trees? I don't think we have one guy over six feet tall."

"Let me explain. There's one hard-to-believe fact about these huge trees. How deep do you think their roots go into the ground?"

The Pressing Champions

Benford scratched his head, looked at me and said, "As big as those suckers are, I'd say their roots go at least 100 to 200 feet in the ground."

I looked at him and smiled. "Actually, their root structure only goes down six to twelve feet deep."

Benford and Curtis looked at me with total misbelief on their faces.

"I know it's hard to believe. Actually, redwoods create their strength to withstand powerful winds and floods by extending their roots more than 50 feet from the trunk and living in groves where the roots can intertwine. In essence, these trees almost totally depend on each other for their rock-solid strong foundation. Individually, these magnificent gigantic trees probably couldn't survive, but collectively, with the assistance of neighboring trees, they thrive.

"The success of our team is very similar because we're going to have to rely on each other with Total Team Togetherness in order to achieve excellence. A continuous full-court pressing defense can only be effective when every player is on the same page. It's my job to create an atmosphere of total aggressiveness. When there's a loose ball, I better see someone diving to the floor after it. A player that does this will get a ton of praise from me, which will send a message to the rest of the team. I am constantly pushing our players real hard in this direction because it is far and away the key to our success."

Coach Johnny Carter

As I headed for class, I looked back at Curtis. "By the way, Curtis, I hope the doubting Thomas you're talking about gets a coaching job somewhere because I'd love for our team to play his team."

We opened the season with back to back games against Apple Springs, our biggest district rival before we moved to Class A. During the warm-up on opening night, Jan Blair, our head cheerleader came over to me and did a complete turnaround.

"How do you like our new cheerleader outfits?"

"Now that's more like it. You look great! Be sure to thank Margie because she did a great job on your uniforms. I definitely approve."

Appreciating my compliment, Jan jogged back over to the other cheerleaders—Linda Wells, Vicki Zalesky, and Betty Curry. They were all smiling when Jan told them what I'd said.

Before the game started, I shook hands with Coach Dick Davidson. He always had his teams highly competitive and we fully expected that to be the case in our first two games. I was surprised at how effective our full-court pressure defense was this early in the season. We won both games with double-digit differences.

Carl Watson did indeed emerge as our fifth starter and his presence was blending in nicely with the other four returning starters. He was quiet and unassuming, but when he was on the floor, his value to our team was obvious. There was a developing similarity resembling our previous teams which was balanced scoring and Carl was a welcome addition because he could definitely score.

Balance was something that I always stressed and felt very good about that ever-developing quality. Pressing teams always rely on total team effort and when you add balanced scoring in the mix, we had something special that was starting to develop. We were a long way from reaching the level of success of our two previous state championship teams, but I was excited about this young team's potential.

The next game on our schedule was the Diboll Lumberjacks, one of the best teams in the state in Class AA. They were coached by one of my best friends and a very good coach, John McGilvra. He had a talented team led by a very athletic 6-foot-8 post man, Mack Mitchell, and an excellent guard, Kelvin Phipps. Although we didn't know it at the time, Mitchell would go on to play football at the University of Houston. He would later be the fifth player taken in the NFL draft by the Cleveland Browns just behind Randy White of the Dallas Cowboys and Walter Payton of the Chicago Bears, two future Hall of Famers.

We definitely had our work cut out for us because there was no way for us to match up with a guy that big. If we didn't get a lot out of our full-court pressure defense, there was no way for us to stay with them. I made this clear to my team in the pre-game talk.

"Look, this team is more talented than we are. On paper, they should kick our butt. Guess what, fellas? Last time I checked, we don't play this game on paper. WE PLAY IT OUT THERE ON THAT COURT. They can draw up all the plays they want on how to get through our press, but then they have to face you guys."

Then, with a slight emerging smile, I said, "Hey, X*s* and O*s* always work on the blackboard, but when you get out there on that court, things are just a little bit different."

The expression on my face was deadly serious, exemplifying the competitiveness within me when I said, "I want to see the most aggressive press that you've ever run in your life out there right now! YOU MAKE THEM EARN EVERY INCH OF THAT FLOOR! You do that and we've got a chance. You don't, then there's no way."

Diboll's strategy was to slow the game down, work the ball into Mitchell and have a low-scoring game. The good news for the Lumberjacks was that they successfully accomplished all three of these objectives, holding us to only 38 points, but their problem was we held them to 31. Our intense pressure defense was absolutely the difference as it caused the Lumberjacks a lot of misery.

After the game, our dressing room was alive with positivity. James Smith came up to me and said, "Pressure D is the key!"

"You got that right, son!"

The Pressing Champions

With a smile, followed by an aggressive fist pump, I said, "Listen up fellas. Congratulations! When you step up the intensity with that kind of total team effort, your potential is limitless. This is the way you have to play for us to be successful. We surprised a lot of people with this win…maybe even ourselves. It's amazing what we can do when everyone THINKS TEAM FIRST! You just found out what it takes to defeat a very talented, well-coached team that has a good chance to go all the way."

As we left the dressing room, Coach McGilvra walked up to me and said, "Well Carter, you got us this time, but we'll be better prepared next time."

I looked at him and said, "You've got a dang good team, incredible potential!"

With a sarcastic smile, he replied, "Yeah, just enough potential tonight to get my butt beat!"

The next day in practice, our confidence level was going right through the roof. We knew that we had defeated a highly ranked team and found out what could be accomplished with super team effort and determination. After practice, Jeff Myers invited me for supper.

"Thanks, Jeff, I'd love to. I've got a few odds and ends to take care of here at the gym before I can leave, but I should be over there in say thirty minutes. Will that work?"

"That's perfect. See you then."

Later, after another great meal, I thanked Mrs. Myers.

"Your meatloaf was absolutely delicious! A single hungry coach always appreciates a home-cooked meal."

She said, "Thanks, we love having you over. You're welcome anytime."

Jeff looked at me. He had a smile on his face.

"Coach, we beat a real good team last night. They've got great talent. That was a huge win."

"They've got all the tools. Give those guys a little more practice time and they're going to be really good."

Harley, Jeff's dad, said, "Coach, you won that game with hustle! It was a total team effort. If we can keep playing like that, we're going to have a great year."

"You're absolutely right, but the keyword is 'if'. There's an old expression, 'If ifs and buts were fruits and nuts, we'd all have a Merry Christmas."

Now everyone was laughing, including me. "Seriously, though, I love the fact that we have to rely totally on all-out effort because that's something that we should be able to do every time we play. It's my job to make sure that we do that every game."

The Pressing Champions

Jeff smiled, but then the look on his face was serious when he said, "As hard as you've been working us in practice, we're going to do that."

"I'm excited about this team's potential because I think our guys realize that's what we have to do to be successful."

Jeff said, "Coach, you've already proved to us in practice that that's the only way our team can be successful. You show that to us every day. Believe me, our guys are sold on pressure defense which requires all-out hustle and you've convinced everyone on our team that's the key for our team doing well."

Illustration by my son, John Carter

Chapter 28
Going Home

Our next game was against Madisonville, my hometown. Having grown up giving my heart and soul to the Mustang basketball program, I was a little bit apprehensive about this game. I'd watched many of the players for the Mustangs grow up and personally knew several of them. I was a huge baseball card collector as a

The Pressing Champions

youngster, as was Tommy Starn, the Mustangs very good point guard.

Tommy may hold the record for mispronouncing the names of baseball players. I will never forget his classic rendition in butchering the names of Ted Kluszewski (Kuskawani), Bill Mazeroski (Makaroni) Early Wynn (Eelie Wine), and Minnie Minoso (Mensow).

As the two teams were warming up, I walked up to Tommy and jokingly said, "I'll trade you a Willie Mays for a Mickey Mantle straight up, no cash involved."

With a laugh, Tommy looked at me and said, "At least I can pronounce those two guys names!" We'd be laughing about this the rest of our lives.

Along with Tommy, the other four starters were Larry Richards, David Garrett, John Sawtelle, and Charles Johnson. I must admit that I had mixed emotions about this game, that is, until the opening tip. Once the game started, those mixed emotions went right out the window because I had a team to coach regardless of who we were playing. We had a distinct advantage. The Mustangs were just finished with football and had had very little practice time. Our aggressive full-court press did indeed give them fits early in the game forcing a much-needed timeout.

In a shell-shocked Mustang huddle, Larry Richards wiped sweat off his brow, looked at Coach James Guess and said, "Coach, what we worked on in practice, it ain't working. It seems like they got seven guys out there going against us."

Coach Johnny Carter

Our team, and in particular, the press, was much farther along this early in the season than I ever imagined. We were starting to do the little things like reacting automatically to a given situation which normally doesn't happen, if at all, until much later in the season. We went on to a convincing 72–44 victory.

After the game, my dad congratulated me and said, "This team is not quite as talented as your two previous state champions, but there's something very unique about how these guys play together so well. Boy, they are fun to watch! They play the game hard and there's definitely no lack of effort out there. I know Coach Guess appreciates the fact that you showed some compassion, called the dogs off, and didn't try to run up the score."

"Why humiliate somebody once the game has been decided? Besides, a lot of those guys are friends of mine. You know a lot of the decisions that I make are a direct reflection of how you and Mom brought me up."

Upon hearing this, Mom gave me a big hug.

"Thanks for being there for me, Mom. I love you guys and appreciate you more than you'll ever know. I'll never be able to repay you for what you've done for me."

My dad looked at me with love in his eyes and looked at Mom, who had that same look in her eyes. Dad put his arm around Mom. They both looked at me and Dad said, "You don't owe us anything, son. We get repaid ten times over every time we look at you."

The next couple of weeks we had return games with both Diboll and Madisonville and the results were about the same as the first contests. Our two senior leaders, Lester and James, continued to be a solid 1-2 punch offensively and defensively, respectively. Whenever we needed a big basket, Lester was the man and James was the key on defense as he virtually made our press very effective. These two guys set the standard with a lead-by-example blueprint for everyone else to follow.

I must admit that I was surprised in our second Diboll game because they decided to play a much faster-paced game. Once again, our press was highly effective and we worked real hard on keeping Mack Mitchell off the boards because we knew he could dominate the rebounding battle. The end result was a 61 to 52 win.

After the game, Coach McGilvra shook my hand and said, "Carter, you run the best press I've ever seen. I thought we were ready for it, but it wasn't in the cards tonight. Even though we lost, it's good for our team to play you because it gets us ready for the tough games coming up down the road."

"I feel the same about playing you guys. It's still early and we both have a lot of practices and games remaining. When it comes time for the playoffs, you'll be there and I honestly think you've got a good chance to go all the way."

John forced a slight smile and said, "Since we don't have to play you guys anymore, maybe so."

The Madisonville tournament was next on our schedule. Ironically, we'd be going against my good friend, Tommy Ferguson, and his potentially good

Chester team. I had previously helped Tommy get this job and he was happy to be back in coaching.

This game would definitely have a hometown flavor because Tommy and I had grown up together. We were great friends, former teammates, and now fierce rivals. Tommy was a relentless competitor and would sometime take it just a little bit too far to the point of getting under your skin.

When we were in high school, I was working in the warehouse of my dad's grocery store and Tommy was working for the Coca-Cola Company. As he came through the warehouse with a dolly of Cokes, he started teasing me about something. I overlooked it for a while, but when he kept on pushing the issue, I got tired of it. Although no punches were thrown, we got into a serious wrestling match. I was a little more athletic than Tommy and I got him in a headlock. Back then, the big deal was to get somebody to give, which meant you won. Squeezing his head with all my might, I shouted, "You give !!!"

"I'll never give!" Tommy shouted back.

Looking to my left, I saw a half empty sack of bulk flour. I promptly stuck Tommy's head in that flour sack. With the sweat covering his face and the butch wax in his hair, the flour stuck to him like a leech. He looked like Casper, the ghost. About that time, Aubrey Standley, Tommy's boss, came into the warehouse and all of a sudden the fight was over.

The Pressing Champions

Aubrey took one look at Tommy and said, "Well, I'll be damned, it's the abominable snowman. Come on, son, we've got to get you cleaned up. I can't let you go to the next store looking like a Hereford."

Tommy tried to talk, but he was still spitting up flour when he said, "What do you mean 'Hereford'?"

Aubrey looked at Tommy, surprised at his question. "You mean to tell me that you grew up in Madison County, which has more cattle per acre than any county in the state of Texas and you don't know what a Hereford is? It's a white face."

I was laughing as they left the warehouse. Showing his never-ending competitive mindset, Tommy looked back at me. With a serious look on his now very white face, he said, "Just remember, Carter, I never gave up!"

That was the last time Tommy ever teased me and we became even closer friends.

The game with Chester turned out to be totally one-sided as we rolled to a 61 to 22 victory. In fairness to Tommy, we had a couple of months extra practice than his team and it showed. Most of his guys played football and it would take a while to get their basketball legs under them. I played my substitutes a lot in the second half, trying not to run up the score.

After the game, Tommy thanked me for showing some mercy. Showing compassion for my friend, I said, "First of all, your team is not nearly as bad as that final score. Second, another month of practice and you'll have an entirely different, highly competitive team."

"I appreciate your confidence. I just wish we could've given you a little better game. It wasn't even a good workout for your team."

As Tommy headed to the dressing room, I knew that he'd use this as a wake-up call for his team and fully expected them to come on strong before this year was over.

Before he got to the dressing room, a local county agent stopped Tommy and with a bit of sarcasm said, "Son, it looks like it's gonna be a long year."

Already very upset by the way his team performed, Tommy snapped back. "I don't know about that, but I do know what you get when you cross an Aggie with an ape."

"What?"

"A hairy county agent!"

This is Tommy's rendition of this story. How truthful it is, no one really knows, but knowing Tommy and how quick he was with comeback lines, I couldn't exclude the possibility. If the truth be known, Tommy probably said, "You're right, sir, we've got a lot of work to do and I can promise you right now, we're going to get a whole lot better!"

Our pressure defense continued to be the dominant force in our overall game with convincing wins over Iola and Huntsville to reach the finals of the tournament against Madisonville. It's hard to beat a team three times, particularly twice on their floor, but that's exactly what we did and extended our record to 11-0.

The Pressing Champions

After handily defeating the Mustangs for the championship, our confidence level was soaring. My team was totally sold on our full-court pressure defense and continued to apply the never-ending, relentless effort required for it to be successful.

In the dressing room after the game, Larry Bruce shook my hand, "How does it feel to beat your hometown team?"

"You know, Larry, during the game, I was totally focused on coaching you guys because that's my job, but now that it's over, I definitely have sentimental mixed emotions. I love this town and this school and have many fond memories of growing up here."

Butch Jones walked up and said, "Coach, you're not saying that you'd feel better if Madisonville had won this game, are you?"

"Are you kidding? I didn't say that, Butch! The past will always be the past, but you know time marches on and Kennard is now where my heart is."

The following week our schedule would continue to have a hometown feel as we were about to travel to Lovelady to play the Lions. Billy Young, another good friend from Madisonville, was the new coach at Lovelady. We'd worked together as lifeguards, commuted together to Sam Houston State University, and just a few years ago took the train all the way to Chicago to see some baseball games.

Like Tommy Ferguson, Billy was a self-made basketball player in high school. What he lacked in talent, he made up for with effort, determination, and a huge passion for the game. In my opinion, these guys make the best coaches because they know what it's like to have to put in the extra hours of work to achieve their goal. It was pretty obvious at the game's outset that our team was much further along than his, mainly because his team, like Chester's, had only been in the gym for a few days after the football season.

This was by far the best that we'd played all year and to make matters worse for the Lions, my team could do no wrong. It was almost scary how well we played.

We shot the lights out, made all our free throws, rebounded well, and the press was the most effective it had been all year. The game was virtually over before halftime.

Trying hard not to embarrass my good friend, I started my second team after the half. To my amazement, my second team played better than my starters. I called timeout, took off the press, and went into a backup, stand-around zone defense.

Late in the game, out of completely understandable frustration, Billy turned around and kicked his ball rack. One of their basketballs rolled down in front of our bench. I picked it up, took it down to their bench and handed it to Billy. To say he was upset would be putting it mildly. He slapped the ball with such force that it bounced about ten feet straight up. I think he now knew what it was like at the Little Big Horn for General Custer. Billy will always be one fierce competitor, but in this situation, there was really nothing he could do. The look in his eye when I shook hands with him after the game said it all.

"Look," I said, "this game is not indicative of how good or bad either one of our teams are. We played way over our head tonight and I know your team is much better than this one game indicates. In fact, I'm gonna predict right now that your team will be in the playoffs this year."

Billy tried real hard to force a smile. "Do you really believe that?"

"I sure do. You've got some good athletes out there. I'm pretty good friends with Tom Nichols, your football coach, and both of his sons, Matt and Mark, are good players.

"Coaches' sons usually have a very competitive mindset and I'm sure those two guys are going to get much better before the year is over. Hunter Allen and Sonny Rollo are also going to be good players for you. You've got the nucleus for a good team. Sometimes a real bad game can ignite the fire deep within.

"Hey, you guys haven't been in the gym long enough. We've been in there since the first day of school. It makes a big difference. I know how much passion you have for this game and I also know what kind of a competitor you are. All you have to do now is transfer some of that to your team and you'll be fine."

"Thanks, Johnny. Right now, in particular, I really needed to hear that."

Coach Johnny Carter

We would play Lovelady two more times and the progress Billy was making with this team became more obvious with each game. Not knowing it at the time, his team would improve dramatically before the year was over. They ended up making it to the regional tournament.

Our early season record had spiraled to 14-0 and our next game would be our second meeting against my good friend, Tommy Ferguson's Chester team. Having grown up with Tommy, I knew the fierce competitor that he was. When we were kids, we played baseball in the backyard using a plastic ball. Tommy had trouble hitting my fastball and invariably I would beat him convincingly. This did not keep Tommy from continually coming back and playing again.

He would call me up and say, "Let's play this afternoon" and I would try to talk Tommy out of playing. "Come on, Tommy! You're no competition, I beat you 15-2 yesterday and that's about as close as you've come since we started playing."

He would come back with, "Yeah, but I've got a new technique that I'm going to use and you'll never beat me again!"

When he said that, I immediately said, "Be at my house at 2 o'clock" and I would pound him again. Even though he lost, he won, because he relentlessly never stopped trying and absolutely would never give up.

The Pressing Champions

I knew how hard he would work his team, particularly trying to beat me. For that reason alone, I knew that this second game would probably be much closer. It was amazing how much better his team played after a lot of work in the gym.

We started the fourth quarter leading by only six points, but then the full-court pressure defense went on a run. Donald Denman started it off with a steal and he quickly hit Lester for a short, spinning two-point jumper.

On the ensuing inbounds pass, as he had done so many times, James deflected the ball. Then Jeff, doing exactly what he was taught, stepped in the passing lane, captured the errant pass and made a perfect bounce pass to Carl Watson for an easy basket. Before Tommy could call timeout, using his God-given quickness, James stole the ball and scored.

In a matter of just 20 seconds, we had exploded for three unanswered baskets, virtually sealing the deal and putting the game out of reach. These types of game changing, quick scoring sequences not only were putting an exclamation mark on many of our games, it was becoming a major part of our team's personality. We ended up winning by a score of 71-56.

After the game, Tommy looked at me with that competitive look in his eye and said, "I thought we had a chance until that press killed us in the fourth quarter. Once you got a couple of steals, it was like it struck a match and ignited your team. When you got that flame started, you fanned it. It was like you poured gasoline on that flame because we went from six behind to fifteen in a flash."

Trying to put a positive spin on the outcome for Tommy, I smiled, looked at him and said, "It's amazing what a few games and two or three weeks of practice have done for the mindset and productivity of your team. You have a totally different team than the first time we played. You've been doing some real BALL coaching, son."

Tommy had that frustrated look in his eye. "Yeah, just enough BALL coaching for you to beat my butt again! At least we gave you guys a better game this time! Man, that is some kind of a press you guys run. It's explosive! You can turn the game around instantaneously! I need to talk to you about that press. I just can't seem to get my guys to execute it as effectively as your team does."

"If you're going home this weekend, let's get together Saturday and we can talk about it."

The following weekend, Tommy came over to our house and we had lengthy discussions about the full-court press. I could tell that he wanted to incorporate it as part of his team chemistry, but was unsure about how to go about it.

"Johnny, the bottom line is that your team is just quicker than mine! I'd love our team to use the press just like your team does, but I don't think we're quick enough to do it?"

The Pressing Champions

"Quickness is a huge factor in the way we play and maybe our style of defense wouldn't work for your team; however, that doesn't mean you can't press. There are lots of ways to run a pressing defense. With your team, I think I would run a more conservative press and not contest the inbounds pass. That way, you can utilize your height and maximize your talent."

I could tell that Tommy wanted to apply inbounds pass pressure, but he conceded that it probably wouldn't work for his team.

"I'm not saying that you never should apply inbounds pass pressure, you just have to limit the number of times that you do it. I'm sure you've probably got some guys on your team that are quick, but just don't play very much. A dead ball press situation would be a good time to get them into the game and change the press."

"Hey, I like that. I could give a couple of guys a short rest."

I looked at Tommy. "You do this and you're gonna look like you're doing some REAL BALL COACHING..." I said, slurring my words.

Tommy started laughing at what I said, but his facial expression quickly became serious. "Thanks, Johnny! I can't wait to put this in. It's gonna help our team a bunch. Tommy had always been a practical joker, but today, for the most part, he'd been dead serious.

Coach Johnny Carter

Our teams would play each other two more times and even though we defeated them all four games that we played, the progression of his team was evident.

The playoff potential with his team was ever so slowly, methodically starting to exemplify Tommy's competitive nature.

Chapter 29

Any Friends Left?

I gazed out the window this mid-December morning while enjoying my first cup of coffee. It was a dreary-looking, early winter day. The sky was gray and there was a definite smell of rain in the air. I was soon joined in the cafeteria by Benford.

"Well, Coach, you're 15-0. That's not a bad start for a young team! You've got to be pleased."

I smiled. "You know when you're totally winning with great effort and that's what I preached to our team from day one, I have no complaints because they're doing exactly what I've asked of them. So far, coaching these guys has been a sheer pleasure and it's not just because we're winning, it's because they're doing the same things in games that we've worked so hard on in practice. You know the old saying, 'Practice what you preach,' well that's exactly what we're doing."

Curtis soon joined us. "So far, Coach, you've whupped Madisonville, Chester, Lovelady, and Diboll, all very good friends of yours. You keep beating up on all your close friends, you're not gonna have any left. You need to play somebody besides all your close friends."

"Man, it's getting dark out there!" said Benford. About that time there was a flash of lightning, followed by a massive thunderbolt which brought on the ensuing rain.

Nona came out of the kitchen and warmed our coffee. "You've got the Crockett tournament this weekend and I'm sure it'll be us against Crockett in the finals. You better not let the Bulldogs beat us!"

Benford looked up and said, "Come on Nona, has Crockett beat us since Coach got here? I don't think so."

"Well, there can always be a first time!"

"Well, that very well may be, but it ain't happening this year!"

I just smiled, glanced out the window at the pouring rain and then headed for my first period class.

The Crockett gym was jam-packed. Just like Nona said, we won our preliminary games and would face the Bulldogs in the finals. Crockett had many incentives to beat us. The fact that bigger schools hate for smaller schools to beat them was not the only reason. When you add that we were undefeated and had won two previous state championships to the mix, that gave them all the motivation they needed to play way above their head. We had motivation, too. We were playing Crockett and most of the people in our little community viewed this as a "must win" game.

As far as I was concerned, this was just another game, but to our fans, it was more than that. Crockett was led by Paul Robbins, Ray Webb, and Jamie Easterly. Jamie, an overall outstanding athlete, was a great pitcher for their baseball team and would be drafted following his senior year by the Atlanta Braves. Later, playing for Milwaukee and Cleveland, he would play major league baseball for 13 years.

When the game started, our pressing defense was too much for Crockett as we started off like a house on fire, took command early, never looked back, and convincingly defeated the Bulldogs 81-50.

Leading up to the Christmas break, our record had swelled to 20–0. I could sense a slight undercurrent of cockiness starting to develop. It's only natural when your team is undefeated for a little bit of this to develop. However, this worried me because it can definitely take you off the main focus. We had won all these games executing a total team concept with everybody doing their part. I didn't want anything to take our mind off of what this team had to do to maintain the momentum that we'd established.

After not being challenged and winning the Centerville tournament, the cockiness was coming to the forefront more and more. With the tough district games just around the corner, this had me concerned. We hadn't had a close game since we played Diboll. I knew we were going to face a lot of competition in our district race. We desperately needed to play someone that would challenge us, maybe even beat us. Since all of our remaining games leading up to district were probably going to be blowouts, I decided to give my friend, John

McGilvra at Diboll a call to see if he had an open date before district started.

To my surprise, John said, "Man, I don't want to play you guys again. Losing both games to you was bad enough, but three times! I don't think so!"

"Look, we both have a tough district schedule coming up and I think this game would be beneficial to both of our teams. Hey, I don't even mind getting beat if it makes our team better!"

John paused for a minute, then said, "I'll play you with one condition. You've got to come over here to play the game."

Without even thinking, I said, "We'll be there."

Honestly, I didn't know if we could beat Diboll a third time, particularly a second time in their gym, but at this point of the season, winning this game wasn't nearly as important as playing against a really good team.

The Holiday season had come and gone. It was January in East Texas and although not as cold as our friends to the north, Texas cold has a personality of its own. Such was the case today as that blistering wicked wind of winter continued dropping the temperature very close to freezing.

Inside the warmth of our little gym, I was discussing an addition to our schedule with my team. "Fellas, we need to play somebody that will challenge us and I've added a game that will do exactly that."

Butch Jones asked, "Who we got, Coach?"

The Pressing Champions

"We've got another game with Diboll. They've improved a lot since we last played them back in November."

Jeff Myers, our point guard, looked at me and said, "Coach, we've also improved a lot, don't you agree?"

"We have improved a lot, but they've got that big guy. They'll give us all we want, maybe more than we want. You'll be playing a team that in my opinion could very well be the state champion of Class AA. I've been telling you for a while that we're not nearly as good as we could be. I'm telling you right now, we could play our best game of the year and still lose this game."

Lester, our lead by example senior, spoke up. "Well, we'll just have to play better than our best game of the year!"

I smiled, looked at Lester and at the team. "That's exactly what we've got to do!"

Jimmy Twine asked, "Where are we playing this game?"

"At Diboll."

Johnny Burson spoke up. "Coach, you told us how hard it is to beat anybody three times and now you're asking us to beat the best team we played all year a second time on their floor? It's almost like you're trying to get us beat."

"Not at all, I'm just trying to get us ready for district. We've had way too many easy games."

Chapter 30
Diboll Again!

An overflow crowd packed the Diboll gym as their very talented team could not wait to avenge the two losses that we had given them earlier. With a playoff type atmosphere, the Lumberjacks played great in the first half and literally kicked our butt. They had a roaring home court crowd and utilized that advantage to its fullest. After having a ton of trouble with our full-court press the first two games, they had a great game plan and executed their new press break with precision.

Headed for the dressing room, we were 11 points behind. This was the first time all year that we trailed at the half. Coach McGilvra commented to the officials as he left the floor, "You guys are doing a great job. That's the best officiating I've had this year."

In our dressing room, to say I was hot was an understatement. Steam was rising from my forehead as I stared at my team! Throwing my purple towel forcefully against the wall, I turned and angrily said, "I've been trying to tell you guys for about three weeks that you're not as good as you think you are and that first half out there proves it. They've beat you in every facet of the game." Then, with a raised voice, I shouted, "If that doesn't make you angry, then I'm about to make you mad. THEY MADE YOU LOOK LIKE A JV TEAM! WE ARE

The Pressing Champions

MUCH BETTER THAN THAT! Now that I've got that anger out of my system, here's what we're gonna do. They're lobbing the ball to the big man to beat our press. He then pivots and looks to pass the ball to a guard on the other side of mid court – not a bad plan. It worked great the first half.

IT AIN'T GONNA WORK THE SECOND HALF! I know that Mack Mitchell is 6-foot-8. We can't do much about that. James Smith, we're going to make a change on our press and I'm putting you on Mitchell."

James had a bewildered look on his face when he said, "Coach, that guy is as big as a house. Are you sure you want me to cover him?"

"I'm positive, son, because we're about to find out if the big guy can dribble the ball. When he gets the ball, I want the rest of you guys to overplay the passing lane on the guy you're guarding. You play hardnose passing lane defense and guess what, we make the big guy dribble the ball and that's one-on-one against you, James. You guys keep your man from getting the ball from the big man and we've got a good chance to win this thing. If you don't...well, they're gonna kick your butt."

Leaving the dressing room, Donald Denman looked at James and asked him how he felt about the second half. "I just hope this change with our press works. How do you feel, Don?"

"I dang sure don't feel like losing! If we do, I don't want to face Coach after the game or as far as that goes, in practice tomorrow either!"

Implementing the change on our press paid dividends early as James Smith made like a bandit, stripping the ball from Mitchell. He then made a quick pass to Carl Watson on the run for an easy bucket. In fact, using his incredible quickness, James stole the ball the next two times from Mitchell, resulting in two more fast-break baskets.

Taking a hint from the popular TV show, "It Takes a Thief" with Robert Wagner, James had helped us turn the tide of this game. Amazingly, we'd cut the lead to five in the first three minutes of the second half and the momentum definitely switched to our side. This forced the Lumberjacks to call a much-needed time-out.

We had totally taken away their confidence as we continued to climb back into the game. Early in the fourth quarter, Lester received a nice pass from Jeff. With a flawless crossover dribble, he penetrated the lane and with a nice pump fake, ripped the cords. This gave us a one-point lead.

Diboll's stunned crowd could only watch in disbelief as we never trailed again, winning by a score of 69 to 61. Naturally upset by the outcome, Coach McGilvra reversed his first half opinion as he commented to the officials, "That's the worst game I've had called all year! I don't want you guys to ever call a game for me again."

As I shook hands with John after the game, I said, "Both of us wanted badly to win this game and needed a game like this. In the long run, it's gonna help both of our teams in the district because it was just like a playoff game. Look, even if we'd lost, I would still be saying the same thing." Though disappointed, John reluctantly agreed.

Our dressing room was alive as our players were enjoying the harvest of our effort. Entering the dressing room, I looked at my team and said, "Congratulations! That was a great come-from-behind win and we desperately needed a game like this because of all the blowouts that we've had up to now."

I'd hoped that this game would diminish some of the cockiness that my team was starting to develop when Jeff Myers walked up to me and said, "Coach, you might as well face it, we're pretty dang good!"

With a semi-smile, I said, "Maybe you're right, son, but you know what, I'm about to work you guys even harder because I don't think we're close to being as good we can be."

"Oh, come on, Coach, we can't play much better than we did in that second half."

With a raised eyebrow, I looked at Jeff and said, "We can always play better! Let's enjoy this great moment, but remember we have some even bigger games coming up. Any questions? If not gather up your stuff and let's go home."

As we got on the bus, Benford looked at me and said, "Well, Coach, you did it again. Another very good friend bites the dust."

Starting the bus, he looked back at me and asked, "Do you have any close friends left?"

Laughing along with him, I said, "I hope so, but you know something, this game is exactly what our team needed. Tonight was a reminder that if we let up just a little bit against a good team, we can easily bite the dust and many of the district games coming up will be just like tonight...maybe even tougher!"

Walking through the hall the next day, Jan Blair stopped to talk to me.

"Great game last night, Coach. Congratulations! We turned that game around in a hurry! How does it feel to be undefeated?"

"It feels great, but our toughest games are still to come with this district schedule."

"You remember right before our first game I told you that I wanted our cheerleaders to do everything within our power to ensure that you had a chance for a perfect season? Well, we've done a pretty good job because right now YOU ARE PERFECT."

Holding my index finger to my lips, I said, "Keep your voice down, Jan. My guys are already pretty cocky and I'm trying to downplay that. It's a day-by-day thing."

"It's pretty hard to downplay that when you're 27-0! I can tell you exactly why we're perfect."

Then, with a laugh she said, "It's because our cheerleaders have done a great job for you."

The Pressing Champions

I laughed with her and said, "You know something, you're absolutely right, but it's gonna be really hard to maintain what we have going. I just want you to know that if we do lose a game, I'm going to blame it on you because you're the head cheerleader and just like with me, the buck stops with the boss. So, don't you girls let up, just keep doing what you're doing."

She walked back down the hall with a smile, turning heads with each step she took given the micro-mini she was wearing.

Our first district game was with Hudson, a suburb of Lufkin. They were coached by Ken Barrington, the architect of a well-coached team. This would be a difficult game for us, not only because of their style of play, but they were much bigger than we were. Hudson was thoroughly prepared, made few mistakes, and would definitely try to keep the score low with their disciplined offense. It would definitely be a hard game for us to win. The game did go down to the final seconds and it took a clutch jump shot by Lester late in the game for us to edge out a 42–39 nail-biting victory.

Scheduling that last game with Diboll was already paying dividends because it prepared us to be ready to play a close game.

Our next opponent would be Groveton, coached by John Reynolds, an outstanding young coach and a good friend.

Coach Johnny Carter

An excellent, all-around athlete growing up there, John went on to play both football and basketball at Texas A&M. He was a member of Coach Shelby Metcalf's 1964 Southwest conference champions. Also on that team were two of my Lon Morris Junior College teammates—Ken Norman of Dallas and Bill Gasway of Burkeville. Another teammate, Eddie Dominguez would join the Aggies the following year.

When the game started, our full-court pressure defense was just too much for the Indians and we won going away, elevating our district record to 2-0. Groveton High School got its nickname from the many Indian tribes that inhabited this area hundreds of years prior to the arrival of the first white settler, Jesse James, in 1844. Interestingly, he was the uncle of two famous western outlaws, Frank and Jesse James, who allegedly visited him frequently, probably when they were on the run.

Another infamous Texas outlaw and gunfighter, John Wesley Hardin, spent his childhood years at Sumpter, which was only five miles from present-day Groveton. Once a boom town, now a ghost town, it was here that he killed his first man at the tender age of fifteen.

Our next game would be against Huntington. The Red Devils had a rich history of basketball success, having previously won three state championships. In fact, my junior year at Madisonville, they beat us by one

The Pressing Champions

point in the playoffs. Nobody came close to them the rest of the way as they easily won the state championship. That game still haunts me because I missed a shot from the corner at the buzzer that probably would have given us an eventual state championship. Presently, we were about to play Huntington again, only this time I was coaching. We completely dominated Coach Jackie Crawford's team start to finish, winning by score of 81-52.

Coming on strong, Carl Watson had a great game as he scorched the strings for a game high 27 points. Lester and James had 14 points apiece, while Donald Denman had 12. Larry Beall led Huntington with 16, followed by Robert Johnson, Jim Shafner, and Walter Johnson with eight points apiece.

Our last game in the first round of district was with Central Consolidated of Pollock, led by their outstanding senior, Carroll Richardson. They also had a previous state championship back in 1956. On that state championship run, they defeated my hometown of Madisonville in a hotly contested, down-to-the-wire contest. I remember going to that game as a grade school kid and was heartbroken. My competitive juices were already flowing then. We definitely had our work cut out for us in our upcoming game with Central because they were one of the best teams in our district.

The day before our game, I got a phone call from John Reynolds, the head coach at Groveton. I could tell by the way he talked that he was angry.

"Johnny, don't you play Central tomorrow night?"

"Yes! I've scouted them twice and they're pretty good."

"Yeah, they're pretty good, but what happened to us the other night was totally uncalled for! Do me a favor! Beat the hell out of them! I've got to tell you what happened in our game. I've had the flu the last three days and actually got out of bed to go coach the game. We only had six players, three starters were missing that were also sick. With foul problems in the fourth quarter, we only had three guys on the floor. Five against three is not very good odds! They didn't call the dogs off, showed no mercy, just kept pounding us even though the game had been over for a long time. To say that I was mad after that game would be an understatement. I told their coach that if I ever had a chance to return the favor, believe me I would, but then without thinking, I said 'Just in case I don't get that chance, I just might drive up to Central and personally whip your ass.'"

I had a semi-smile on my face because knowing the competitor that John was, this was not a surprise.

"I'm sorry that you've been sick. Are you back at school?"

"Today is my first day back."

"What happened in your game is something that doesn't have to be. My starters sometimes get upset with me when I take them out early. Sometimes coaches get so obsessed with their own team that they fail to show any compassion for their opponent."

The Pressing Champions

"That's the way that you and I look at it. Unfortunately, that's not the case with all coaches. Anyway, you've got a better team than Central. Good luck in your game.

"Thanks John, I appreciate that and I'm glad you're feeling better."

Coach Wyatt Dotson always seemed to have a very competitive team and this year was no exception. Before another overflow home crowd stimulating our full-court pressure defense, we managed to escape with a 59-52 win. James, Lester, and Carl netted 17, 15, and 14 points, respectively, in leading our scoring parade.

Johnny Grimes scored 17 for Central, followed by Carroll Richardson and Curtis Aldredge with 13 each. We were still undefeated for the season, but more importantly, undefeated through the first round of our district schedule.

It was a clear, bright, sunshiny morning as I was back at in the cafeteria having my first cup of coffee. I was soon joined by Curtis, who had been a big asset to me by scouting teams that we would be playing.

"Good morning, Coach. Well, how do you feel about the first half of district?"

"I was really worried about it before we started district play because I knew we would have some really close games. Other than Diboll, we've really had no close games all year and that just doesn't prepare you for a highly competitive game. The third game over at Diboll couldn't have come at a better time. It just may have saved our season."

"I agree. You really don't know how to win a close game unless you experience some of them."

Miss Nona came out of the kitchen and warmed our coffee. "Well, Coach, you're 32-0. Has it surprised you how well this team has played so far?"

"We've won all those games with great effort and honestly, that hasn't surprised me because I see that in practice every day. The fact that we haven't lost a game definitely surprises me."

As she walked away, she looked back and said, "What do you think is the key to the success of our team?"

I smiled, looked at her and answered. "Well, obviously the full-court press, but aside from that, it's unselfish togetherness. Individually, I'm getting what I expected out of Lester and James, maybe a little more than expected. Carl Watson and Donald Denman just keep getting better every day. I like balance and these four guys are all averaging in double figures. Jeff could be also, but that's not his job. He's probably the backbone of our team because he just plain makes everybody else better. He's the perfect point guard for this team. When you add the off-the-bench contributions of Larry Bruce and Butch Jones, it makes for a pretty good all-around team."

The Pressing Champions

She stopped, then walked back to the table. She looked at me and said, "We know who the real backbone of this team is and I'm looking at him!"

"Thanks, I do appreciate that, but you know what? I haven't scored one point this year, haven't got one rebound or one steal off the press. I think you're just a little bit prejudiced."

As she walked away, she replied, "Yes, I am."

Waiting for the first period class to begin, I was talking to Donald Denman, our junior post man. "Donald, I was talking to Truman Lamb and he told me that you were raising a calf for the Houston fat stock show."

"Yes sir, I was chosen to compete in a calf scramble down there last year and managed to get a calf. I'm obligated to raise it for the show this year."

With a smile, I said, "I bet your quickness helped you get that calf."

Donald chuckled. "It probably did."

I laughed as I said, "No wonder you're so good on the press. You've had a lot of practice chasing that calf."

About that time, I looked down the hall and saw Donald's absolutely beautiful sister, Deborah, coming up the hall.

"Good morning, Deborah."

"Hello, Coach." With a shy smile, she said, "Don't let up on my brother. He needs all the coaching you can give him!"

Coach Johnny Carter

As she walked away, I looked at Donald, glanced back at her and then said to him, "So you and Deborah are twins? Man, she is gorgeous! What happened to you?"

"Come on, Coach, that's not fair! You can't be comparing a girl to a guy."

Now we were both laughing. "I'm sorry, Donald, but you know what, I can be kinda blunt. I just tell it like it is."

With that come-back look in his eye, he said, "Well you're right about one thing, she did get all the looks, but you know what...I got all the speed. I can outrun her big time!"

We both laughed. "You're right about that, son. You move so fast out there on that floor, you're like a blur and I can't really tell how much better looking she is than you! So, do me a favor...keep running fast, son."

We were both snickering as we headed to first period class.

The Pressing Champions

Hudson, who gave us all we wanted the first time, would be our opponent in the first game of the second round. In the dressing room prior to this game, I was speaking to my team.

"Get ready for another close game. These guys did a great job against us the first time and with their conservative approach, I'm expecting a similar game this time.

"Don't let up on the press because just about the time you think that it's not working, it will find a weakness, allowing us to break a game wide open. That's the beauty of our style of play, so whatever you do, keep up the pressure.

"Look, they'll try to rock you to sleep with their offense, so you've got to show that same relentless intensity when we play half-court defense as we do on the press. They want to control the tempo of the game. It's your job to not let that happen. Okay, let's have our prayer."

Our little gym was jam-packed to the rafters, giving us an earthquake-like ovation as we took the floor. People were sitting along the sidelines on the floor. It was standing-room-only behind the seats on the stage. The exits were crowded with many of our late arriving fans unable to find a seat. Because our first game with Hudson was so close, they were expecting another barnburner, unlike most of our games this year.

In comparison, voters in our democratic election process are much like hometown fans. They make a choice at the ballot box and are only satisfied when their candidate wins. It's virtually the same with most hometown fans. We had totally spoiled them because they had not seen a loss all year. The progression of our team changed many of our fans' low expectations at the beginning of the year to thinking that we were now unbeatable.

Just like the first game, Hudson gave us all we wanted and even though we were in command most of the way, we never could secure a comfortable lead. Utilizing the speed that I had earlier ribbed him about, Don Denman had an exceptional game, particularly on our press. In the end, we had another low-scoring contest, escaping with a 49-43, fan-pleasing, hard fought victory.

I couldn't help but congratulate Donald after the game "Great game, son! You were all over that floor. You moved so fast out there that I didn't even notice how much better looking your sister is than you."

Out of the corner of his eye, but with a sly smile, he said, "You're never going to let that die, are you, Coach?"

As we walked into a celebratory dressing room, I looked at him, smiled, and said, "Nope."

Our unbeaten streak continued as we soundly defeated Groveton and Huntington, leading up to our final district game against Central. They were a well-

The Pressing Champions

coached team and we were expecting another close game.

Carroll Richardson, a seasoned senior and one of their best players had been on the varsity all four of his high school years. Keeping him below his average was a key for us to win this game. We had defeated them by seven points in the first round and were expecting another highly contested game.

An overflow capacity crowd filled their gym for this championship-deciding game. James and Lester, our two senior leaders, scored 18 apiece in leading us to a 75-68 victory. With Carl and Donald scoring 14 and 13 respectively, we again had four players in double figures. Jeff dished out assist after assist, giving us a total team victory. Carroll Richardson scored 18 to lead Central, followed by Robert Luce with 17 and Johnny Grimes with 12.

Chapter 31
The Playoffs

Entering our joyful dressing room, I had all the players sit down in front of me while I gave my post-game talk.

"First of all, congratulations on this great year so far. You've played far better than most people thought you were capable of doing and it's all because of your great effort.

"Don't ever forget how we got to this point. We just flat out-hustled the teams we played and now we start a brand-new season. It's the playoffs and guess what? We have a best two-out-of-three rematch with the **Alto Yellow Jackets.**

"Most of you were on the team last year when they eliminated us from playoffs. Fellas, it's payback time. It's your chance to turn the tables and eliminate their playoff run. It won't be easy because they're good—every bit as good as they were last year. I've got news for them, we're a lot better than we were last year!"

There was rousing, energetic, enthusiastic approval! When the reaction simmered down, I continued.

"We'll play the first game Friday in Crockett, the second game Tuesday at Rusk, and if a third game is needed, we'll play in Palestine on Thursday or Friday."

The Pressing Champions

James spoke up. "We ain't going to need a third game, Coach. We're gonna take care of those guys in two games."

"I hope you're right, James. That would be great, but I promise you it's not going to be easy."

Lester, our lead-by-example senior, spoke up. "Coach, they're not going to beat us again. We're going to get after them like they've never seen us before!"

I smiled as I left the dressing room because, if for no other reason, we had a mindset in a very positive direction.

Our practices the next two days were incredibly intense. We were totally focused and seemed to be on an all-out mission to avenge last year's playoff loss. Full-court pressure defense had been our bread-and-butter all year long and we continued to work on it daily. We had an extremely hard practice on Wednesday and lightened up a bit the next day.

Cutting practice a little short, we were near the end and shooting free throws. After rotating back-and-forth, shooting one and one free throws, I said, "Okay, everyone on this end and on the line. Lester, you're on the free-throw line. You're shooting a one and one. Make the first, you get a second. If you miss, it's five sprints for everyone. If you make the first and miss the second, it's three sprints. You make them both and guess what? We go to the house."

Coach Johnny Carter

I handed him the ball and made like a play-by-play announcer.

"Hutcherson at the line for a one an one. His team trails by one, there's no time left on the clock, it's all up to him. Listen to that crowd."

Standing close to Lester, I mimicked crowd noise. Lester didn't even smile. He was totally focused, eyed the basket, and ripped the cords. With his teammates responding, I continued.

"Hutcherson has made the first of a one and one to tie the game. He has one more for the win. Lester eyes the basket, bends the knees, and flips the wrist. It's good! It's good! The Tigers win and you guys can go home!"

I had a short team meeting in the dressing room before releasing them. I reminded everyone of the athleticism of the Yellowjackets. "They're a very talented bunch and we're going to have to play our best to get the job done. They won their zone going away and really nobody challenged them. So, we have two teams going against each other that totally dominated district play. It should be a great game. I have a lot of respect for Pat Centilli, their coach. He's a good guy and an excellent coach. You guys get a good night's rest. We have an awfully big game coming up and I want you to be fresh. See you guys tomorrow."

The Pressing Champions

It was early Friday morning as I tried to enjoy my first cup of coffee. It seemed like there were a million things on my mind. Miss Nona came out of the kitchen and handed me a plate with a warm apricot fried pie.

"Coach, you look a little bit uptight. You ought to be feeling great. You're going into the playoffs with a 36-0 record!"

Aw, Miss Nona, I do feel great about our team, it's just you don't want to lose a game at this juncture. It's bad enough to lose a regular season game, but as we found out last year, when you lose a playoff game, the season is over! Like it or not, that's what we're going to be facing every game from now on. I'm just talking to you right now and there's no way I'm going to dwell on this with my team because they couldn't be more positive than they are right now. I want to keep it that way. You know when we played Diboll the third time in their gym, I honestly didn't think that we could go over there and beat them again. When we did it, I was surprised. Diboll had been playing great since we defeated them back in November. They are far and away the best team that we played all year. That game shocked their fans, as well as a lot of ours."

Now she was smiling. "It didn't shock me. It's amazing how much better our team is right now compared to back when the season started. Their togetherness and overall teamwork is as good as any of your previous teams. Regardless of what happens from here on out, what you've done with this team is totally amazing."

"Thanks, I really appreciate what you're saying. Now, if only we can play as good as this fried pie tastes!"

Miss Nona was chuckling as she headed back into the kitchen.

A capacity crowd filled the Crockett High School gym. Electricity filled the air as these two playoff-driven teams with one common goal were about to face-off against each other. The talent-laden Alto Yellowjackets, led by an outstanding player, Larry Jenkins, were attempting to derail our undefeated team.

On the other hand, we would be attempting to erase the memory of last year's devastating playoff loss. From the outset, we controlled the game as our full-court press took its toll on the shell-shocked Yellowjackets. It was all business on our part as our inspired team rolled to a 72-52 hustling playoff victory over the surprised Alto cagers. It was an obvious, total team effort with everyone doing their part.

An incredible feeling of satisfaction engulfed my team as we headed toward the dressing room. When I shook hands with Coach Centilli, he said, "Man, you guys played great tonight. That press totally took us out of the game. I can promise you we will be much better in the second game."

"Believe me, I know that and I'm expecting a much closer game on Tuesday."

The Pressing Champions

Before I got off the floor, Curtis stopped me. "Payback is sweet, right Coach?"

My facial expression told him how I felt without my having to say a word.

Entering a joy-filled dressing room, Jeff Myers shook my hand and said, "How about that game, Coach? We played great! I don't know if we can play any better than that."

With that, Lester stepped in. "Hang on, Coach. I've got this. We can always play better."

Now Jeff, Lester, as well as the rest of the team were all laughing with me while celebrating this huge victory.

Walking down the hall between classes on Monday, Jan Blair came up to me.

"Well, Coach, we are still perfect! How about our Tigers?"

"Would you stop using the word 'perfect'? Hopefully, we've got several games left. If we're still undefeated at the end of the season, then you can say that word all you want."

"Okay, it's a deal, but you and I both know why we're doing so great this year, right?"

"I know, I know, how could I not know? You've reminded me every time I see you! However, I have to admit your cheerleaders are doing great. You better keep it up because like I told you before, if things don't go right, I'm blaming you girls."

We were both laughing as she walked away.

Before practice, I was addressing our team. "Look, you convincingly beat another talented team, but I'm telling you right now, this second game will be totally different than the first one. You woke them up from a deep sleep and I can guarantee you that their coach will have their engine revved up and ready to go tomorrow night. They'll be like a bear coming out of hibernation. Whatever you do, don't judge this next game by the last one."

Larry Bruce asked, "What do you think they'll do different, Coach?"

"That's a good question, Larry. I look for them to do a much better job against our press because it dominated them. They're too good to let that happen again. I really don't care what changes they make because we're going to do what got us here. That's the beauty of the full-court press. It will find and exploit weaknesses. It's been that way all year and we're not going to change what we're doing. Okay, let's have a good practice and get ready for tomorrow."

We had an extremely efficient practice, preparing our game plan for tomorrow. Near the end of practice on a rebounding drill, James Smith came down wrong on his foot. My heart sank as I rushed over to check him out. He assured me that it was no problem. I told him to ice it down as soon as he got home.

The next morning, my heart sank when I saw James get off the bus. He had a slight limp which was not a good sign.

The Pressing Champions

"How's the foot, James? Looks like you're limping a little bit."

"It's a little sore, Coach, but it's going take a lot more than a little soreness to keep me from playing tonight."

Even though James felt like he'd be okay, that little limp had me worried. He made our press go with his great speed and quickness and anything reducing that would definitely hurt our team. I went through the rest of the morning wondering just how effective he'd be tonight.

At lunch, I noticed he was still limping slightly. I was hoping and praying that it would loosen up before the game, but to say I was worried was an understatement. As a coach, you always worry about injuries and we had been blessed all year without any major ones. In my mind, I began thinking what my plan would be if he couldn't go. Since we didn't have anybody that could come close to matching what he did for our defense, we had a problem!

After lunch, I got James out of class and we went into the gym.

"Go put your game shoes on. I want to see what you can do."

It was pretty obvious that he was going to be restricted in his movement. He assured me that by game time he'd be ready. I didn't tell James, but I was preparing myself to approach this game without him. It wasn't a feeling that I was comfortable with.

Coach Johnny Carter

The bus ride to Rusk seemed to take forever. Each member of our team had a special role and James had one of the biggest. I'd built this team around full-court pressure defense and there's no doubt about it, he was our number one presser. I had James sitting beside me on the bus and told him I would tape his ankle when we got to the gym.

Later, in the dressing room, I was just getting ready to tape his ankle when there was a knock on the dressing room door. Carl Watson said, "Coach, there's a man out there who wants to talk to you."

When I got to the door, I was surprised to see an old friend who just wanted to say hello. This guy was an absolute answer to a prayer because he just happened to be a chiropractor. When I told him of my dilemma, he said, "Let me look at your guy."

He checked James out, worked on his foot with some of his chiropractic skills, and the next thing I knew, James was walking around with no limp.

"Coach! My foot is much better. It feels great. I'm ready."

I breathed a major sigh of relief!

"Thank you, thank you, thank you!" I said to my friend. "You may have saved our season."

When we started warming up, I watched James closely and surprisingly, he looked almost normal. I'd been saying a prayer before we started warming up that he'd be able to be himself and the way he looked, that prayer has been answered.

The Pressing Champions

When the game started, I couldn't help but focus on James and how he responded with his movement. Surprisingly, he looked good with little, if any, limping. Obviously, Alto was much better prepared for the second game because they stayed right with us. It was a highly competitive game with the score flip-flopping quite a bit in the first half. James played well, which was surprising to me given his injury.

Alto certainly gave us all we wanted. We did get a slight edge in the second half, but not a big lead. Our press wasn't as effective as it was in the first game, but we expected that and when you combine that with a poor shooting night, this game could go either way.

However, Carl Watson did take up the slack, making one big basket after another, scorching the cords for 24 points. Up by two late in the contest, we were running our sure thing delay game. With a nice back door cut, we got the ball to Lester. He took the ball to the glass and using a nice Hollywood-type pump fake, put up a soft short bank jumper which circled around the rim before stretching the strings for two.

This basket electrified our crowd and sent us on to a 60-56 win. It was Lester's 19th point of the game, followed by Donald Denman with 12. Larry Jenkins was the only Alto player to score in double figures, hitting a game high 26 points.

This was the type of game that every team that goes deep in the playoffs sooner or later will have to win. We had just escaped with a breathtaking down to the wire finish. Curtis was the first guy to offer me congratulations. "Great job, Coach! This team amazes me! Even though we haven't had many close games, this team just seems to rise to the occasion when they have one!"

"Thanks, Curtis. By the way, I do appreciate all your help."

"You know, Coach, I want to be a coach and I've watched every game closely, observing how you went about your business. So far, you've made all the right moves. There is one decision that far surpasses all the others and that was playing Diboll that third time."

"Curtis, that was a no-brainer for me because it was going to help us, even if we lost. At that time, we weren't ready to play a close game because we hadn't had any. I knew this district race was going to be tough and you see how many close games we've had recently."

Curtis smiled. "Six out of our last eleven!"

James Smith met me at the dressing room door. "What did I tell you, Coach? We only needed two games."

"Thank the Lord that the chiropractor just happened to be at our game. That was no coincidence! The Good Lord was looking after you, James. Matter of-fact, He was looking after our team."

"You got that right, Coach! I was thanking Him before the game ever started. I played a little soft at the beginning until out of habit I had to make a hard cut without thinking. After that, I forgot about my injury and just played the game."

The Pressing Champions

"And you played very well, son. That was a hard-fought, down-to-the-wire victory. It was especially gratifying after what they did to us last year, right James?"

"You got that right, Coach! This is my last year and there was no way we were going to let those guys beat us again. Lester and I made a pact last year that this year would be different."

"Well, you guys just keep doing what you're doing and keep encouraging the younger guys."

Our next opponent in the playoffs would be Troy High School, which is located in central Texas near Temple. Despite the fact that Troy had a major height advantage, it was pretty obvious early on that our press was going to give them trouble.

We had a big lead by half-time and cruised to a convincing 64–37 victory over the Trojans, thus qualifying for the upcoming regional tournament.

Lester had another big night scoring 22 points, followed by Don and Carl with 12 points each. Ralph Huber and Ed Newman scored 15 and 12, respectively, for Troy. With this decisive victory, we elevated our record to 39-0, but more important was the fact that we were now just two wins away from going back to the state tournament.

Later in my career, when I coached basketball at McLennan Community College in Waco, we had a great pitcher on our baseball team from Troy. His name was Craig McMurtry.

I made a call to the Chicago White Sox to recommend him and was absolutely blown away when Bill Veeck, their famous future Hall of Fame owner, answered the phone. "May I speak to Mr. Veeck?"

"You got him. Can I help you?"

"You mean you answer the phone?"

"Man, I do it all around here! What can I do for you?"

After getting over the fact that I was shell-shocked by who I was talking to, I finally regained my composure and started telling him why I'd called. When I mentioned the fact that I was calling from Waco, Texas, he immediately interrupted me and said, "Craig McMurtry, 6-foot-5, great prospect, and we don't have a chance to get him because he'll be one of the top three or four players taken in the draft. He'll be long gone before we get to make our selection."

"I'm sorry. I'm just wasting your time." "You're not wasting my time. It's guys like you that put us onto players every day. I'm just glad you're a White Sox fan and thought of us first. Feel free to call us anytime."

Mr. Veeck was right on because Craig was the fourth player taken in the MLB draft, the number one draft choice of the Atlanta Braves.

The Pressing Champions

Chapter 32
The Regional Tournament

As I gazed out the window in the cafeteria the next morning, I had the regional tournament on my mind. This tournament would be held at Blinn Junior College in Brenham, the county seat of Washington county.

Many years ago, just up the road was the busy riverboat town of Washington-on-the-Brazos, so named to distinguish the settlement from Washington-on-the-Potomac (i.e., Washington, DC.) As the Alamo was about to fall to Santa Anna's army, history was made there on March 1, 1836, when delegates convened and declared Texas' independence from Mexico.

These brave men literally were signing their own death warrant because they had no idea that General Sam Houston's Army would defeat Mexico in the battle of San Jacinto. Washington on the Brazos would be the capital of Texas from 1842 to 1845 when it was relocated to Austin. The signal for the demise of this town came about when riverboats were replaced by railroads.

Miss Nona came to my table and warmed up my coffee. "Great game last night, Coach and another total team effort."

Thanks, Miss Nona. That's what our team is all about. When you get right down to it, that's a basic prerequisite for the press. If you don't have that, running a continuous full-court press defense is a waste of time."

"Well, obviously you're not wasting your time because your defense is eating people alive! Speaking of the press, here comes one of the main reasons why it's been so successful."

I looked up and Donald Denman was walking toward my table with a rather disturbed look on his face.

"Coach, I need to talk to you, in private." We walked down to my classroom and closed the door.

"What's on your mind, son? You look worried!"

"I've got a problem and I've been scared to tell you."

"I told you guys a long time ago to always feel free to come talk to me about anything. So, what's up?"

"Coach, remember when I told you that I was raising a calf for the fat stock show? Well, that show is this week and I'm obligated to show the calf in Houston. I signed the paperwork and gave my word that I'd bring my calf to Houston and show it. What can I do, Coach?

"Do you know what your schedule is this week?"

"I'm not really sure, but I'm supposed to be in Houston today with the calf. I don't know what to do, Coach. I can't miss the regional tournament."

"Go get your schedule. I want to look at it and see if there's anything we can do."

As he left to go get his schedule, I had a sinking feeling for the second time in the last few days. First it was James maybe not getting to play in our second Alto game and now Donald's availability for regional was in question! So many things have to go right in order to achieve what we were trying to do and now we have another obstacle.

After looking at Donald's schedule, I told him to let me work on this and maybe I can work something out. "I think there might be a way that you can show your calf and also play in the regional tournament. Go on down to Houston and show your calf. You need to honor your commitment and don't worry about missing practice. In this case, you're excused."

"Thanks, Coach. Please work this out. I can't miss regional. We're too close to getting back to Austin."

"Good luck in Houston."

I walked back down to the cafeteria to get one last cup of coffee, wondering what I was going to do about Donald's situation. The door opened and Curtis walked in.

"Coach, you don't look like someone who just won a big playoff game."

"I have a problem."

When I explained to him the situation, he immediately said, "Coach, we've got to have Donald. Is there anything I can do?"

"Thanks, Curtis. I appreciate your thoughtfulness."

Handing me a newspaper, he said, "I see we play Lexington in the first game of regional on Saturday morning."

"Are you sure it's not Friday?"

"The paper says we play Saturday at 10 a.m.

"So, we might have to play two games on Saturday. The style of a ball that we play, that's a big disadvantage. On the other hand, right now that just might be an answer to a prayer."

"Curtis, there may be something you can do. I think Don shows his calf on Friday. Could you go to Houston and bring him to Brenham?"

"Absolutely."

"Great! Thanks so much, this may save us."

As I walked to my first period class, my stress level, which was already pretty high because of the playoffs, was eased just a little bit.

Four teams from Class A, as well as AA, were on their way to Brenham, Texas having qualified for the regional tournament. Just as I had predicted and to no one's surprise, Diboll would also be there. As we traveled south to Brenham, there was a trickling of the annual emergence of bluebonnets, the state flower of Texas.

The Pressing Champions

In two or three weeks, the landscape would be a gorgeous pictorial sea of blue. Brenham was also the home of a small up-and-coming company with a product that was about to explode with popularity—Blue Bell Ice Cream.

Illustration by my son, John Carter

Besides our first-round opponent, Lexington, the other two teams were Malakoff and West Sabine, a perennial basketball power with two previous state championships. Last year, West Sabine reached the state finals against Friendwood, ironically the team that we defeated for the state championship two years ago.

All the experts predicted that we would play West Sabine in the regional finals.

A couple of hours before our game with Lexington, Jeff and Lester were approached by two guys from West Sabine. "Are you guys from Kennard?"

Jeff replied, "Yes."

Coach Johnny Carter

"Well, you better not lose because we can't wait to give y'all your first loss!"

Normally soft-spoken, Lester had his competitive juices surge to the forefront when he replied, "Then you better not let Malakoff beat you!"

We were in the dressing room, just starting to get dressed. Donald Denman was nowhere to be seen. In my mind, I was preparing for us to play this game without him. Curtis was supposed to be here with him long before now. I was wondering if something had gone wrong. Pondering how to approach this, I said a silent prayer. I could feel the apprehension in the room.

After everyone was dressed, I had them sitting before me and was about to tell them how we were going to approach this game without Donald when suddenly the dressing room door opened and in walked Curtis and Donald.

Immediately, the tension in the room was lifted and there was a relieved look on the faces of my players.

Curtis said, "I'm sorry we're late, Coach. We got into a major traffic jam just outside of Houston."

"Man, I'm just glad you guys are safe and sound. Hurry up and get dressed, Donald. Come out and join the warm-up as quick as you can."

As Don hurriedly got dressed, our warm up drills prior to the game went smoothly. Our opponent was from Lexington, a town located some 45 miles northeast of Austin. It's named after Lexington, Massachusetts, site of the first battle of American Revolutionary War.

The Pressing Champions

When the game started, I was really surprised at how well Donald played because he had literally slept in the barn with his calf the last few nights and he was tired before the game even started. Despite that, Donald scored 19 points while getting numerous steals off our press, leading us to an overwhelming 75-52 victory. It was one of his best games of the year. Carl and James added 16 and 14, respectively.

**Team Huddle 1970
Regional Finals, Brenham**

Our aggressive pressing defense basically took its toll, clipping the wings of the high-flying Eagles and forcing numerous turnovers. They were led in scoring by Larry Carothers with 19 and Dennis Taylor with 13, but it wasn't nearly enough to overcome our intense overall team play. Congratulating my team in the dressing room, I shook hands with Donald.

"Son, you played great. You moved so fast out there that guess what, I didn't come close to noticing how much better-looking Deborah is than you."

Donald rolled his eyes and said, "Man, I'm dead tired, but I did play pretty good, didn't I, Coach?"

"You better believe it, son! I'm just glad you made it to the game. By the way, I have a between games plan just for you. We have a motel for the rest of the guys, but I have Mr. Frizzell looking for a barn with a haystack for you. The way you played this morning, I want a repeat performance tonight. Why change something that's working?"

Donald and I were both laughing, as was the rest of the team.

West Sabine couldn't wait to play us in the regional finals, but they forgot about one important obstacle. They had to beat Malakoff first. They were playing us in the finals before they ever played Malakoff. That turned out to be a big mistake because they were upset in their semi-final game. We were now one game away from going back to Austin and our opponent would be Malakoff, a community approximately 80 miles southeast of Dallas.

This town is named after the Russian fort of Malakoff, which played a pivotal role with the British/French siege of Sebastopol during the Crimean war in 1855. The central theme of this conflict was the vicious trench fighting which took place. This was a foretaste of how the American Civil War would be fought

The Pressing Champions

ten years later and finally World War I, which began in 1914.

Lester was particularly upset that we weren't going to play West Sabine. He looked at Jeff during our lunch and said, "Dang it! I wanted to play those guys. The only way to shut them up is to play them."

Jeff looked at Lester and smiled. "Malakoff shut them up for us."

Lester responded with "Yeah, but I wanted our team to do it."

"Man, we can't worry about their loss. We've got more important business to take care of tonight."

The regional finals were now set. We would play Malakoff for the Class A Championship at 7 o'clock. Diboll and Kountze would meet in the AA final at 8:30. Two of these teams would be on their way to Austin next week in quest of a state championship, while the other two would go home heartbroken. We were resting between games at the same motel as Diboll and I was visiting with my good friend, Coach John McGilvra.

"Well, John, congratulations! You've had a heckuva year. I knew you'd be here. Just one more victory and we'll both be in Austin."

"That would be great, but unfortunately, the thing that you said that bothers me the most was just one more victory!"

We both laughed. "I've already been involved with two regional final games and they were both laughers."

Coach Johnny Carter

John looked at me with a curious look on his face. "You mean you won both of those games real easy?"

Sarcastically, I said, "Oh yeah, real easy. We won both games by one point! I can laugh about them now, but I dang sure didn't laugh about them then."

With a cautious laugh, John said, "Dang, Carter! I was already a little nervous before I started talking to you and what you said just now has not eased my nerves at all."

Now we were both laughing. "Listen, John, just enjoy the fact that you're here. You're one game away from the state tournament. You remember last year when along with Tommy Ferguson we watched the state tournament together?"

"I remember," Tommy said, 'Wouldn't it be great if all three of us brought our teams to the state tournament this year?' Well, we're one game away from getting there and Tommy's team has qualified for regional next week in San Marcos."

John and I had a sentimental look in our eyes pondering that possibility. We were both smiling when I said, "Think about all the coaches that would love to be in our shoes right now. We worked hard to get to this point and right now we're exactly where we want to be. So, let's just relax and enjoy where we are. Let me give you some advice. Right now, you need to become an actor because you don't want your players to think that you're nervous. It's okay to be nervous, just don't act like you are. You want your players to do exactly what they did to get your team to this point, so lay back, relax, and enjoy the moment."

"Thanks for the encouragement, but I'm still a little nervous."

"Hey, so am I, but when I go into that dressing room tonight, I'm going to become Robert Redford."

John was laughing when he said, "Well, I'm not good looking enough to be Robert Redford, maybe Robert Stack."

Now I was laughing. "Hey, when he played Elliot Ness in that award-winning TV show, *The Untouchables* he took down Al Capone and guess what? In the end, he always won. That's what I want you guys to do tonight. Good luck, John."

"You too, Carter."

We started the game with Malakoff on a high note as the intensity of our full-court pressure defense paid big dividends the first quarter and had us leading 19 to 12. That was about to change in the second quarter when some unforeseen circumstances vastly altered our productivity.

In the huddle, Jeff Myers, our point guard looked at me and said, "Coach, my stomach is killing me!"

Despite the fact that Jeff told me he could play, I decided to give him a break. During the next free-throw break, Carl Watson came over to the bench with a painful look on his face, pointing to his stomach, so I took him out too. All of a sudden, early in the game, we had two of our starters on the bench and this vastly changed the complexion of the game.

After an impressive first quarter, we scored only seven points in the second, leading by only 26-20 at half time. We were in trouble! I knew it and our team could sense it. Our fans had no idea of what was going on. I hoped and prayed that our halftime break would help us regain normalcy.

I'd never seen Donald get tired, but what he'd gone through the last three or four days, not to mention his superb effort in this morning's game, he literally was operating on fumes.

"Are you okay, Donald? You look exhausted."

"Coach, I've never been this tired in all my life!"

"Can you go the second half, son?"

"I've got to, Coach. The team needs me. I'll be okay."

This halftime break couldn't have come at a better time. Despite what he said, I knew I had to watch him closely, knowing that I might have to give him a break at some point in the second half. What I didn't know at the time was that Donald's dad had come to the game and Don was probably trying too hard. His dad seldom got to see him play and this added more pressure to an already stressful situation.

Jeff and Carl convinced me that they could go the second half, so we started the second half with all of our starters. At least for the moment, this proved to be the right decision because we increased our lead at the end of the third quarter to 45-34.

Almost every game of the season we had four or five guys score in double figures; however, in this game, almost all of our scoring had come from our two senior leaders, Lester and James. It's a good thing that we increased our lead because the stomach problems came back in the fourth quarter and I had to bench Carl and Jeff several times. This triggered a major momentum shift and when Donald fouled out, it just fueled the fire.

Having upset West Sabine in the morning semi-final, Malakoff now had the wind to their back and they were sensing another huge upset. They were attempting to become the Cinderella team of the tournament.

With less than one minute left in the game, our lead had been reduced to one point and we could feel this one slipping away. Attempting to put out the fire, we were running our delay game and with just a few precious seconds left, Larry Bruce was fouled and sent to the charity stripe.

The Kennard faithful behind us were on the edge of their seats, sensing what might possibly be our first loss, thus ending this incredible season. With the outcome of this game riding squarely on his shoulders, Larry, our left-handed junior, eyed the bucket, bounced the ball three times, bent his knees and flipped his wrist.

His soft-spinning one-hander looked good leaving his hand and when the ball came down, it ripped the cords, sending our very partial fans into a frenzy. We ended up winning this nail-biter 54-50 in a game which saw our opponent almost pull off their second huge upset of the day.

Fortunately, Lester swished the strings for 20 points with James following close behind with 18, leading us to this state tournament qualifying victory. Malakoff was led by Elbert Sparks, Robert Reed, and Jesse Green with 17, 15, and 13, respectively.

This game was filled with adversity totally beyond our control and yet we somehow managed to rise above all of the negativity and pull off as of now the biggest win of the year.

As I walked off the floor, I could see that my dad had a look of relief on his face.

"Son, you about gave me a heart attack. Congratulations! This team just seems to do what it has to when everything is on the line. You've had that competitive spirit about you all your life and you've transferred that mindset to your teams. You're about to go back to Austin for the third time in the last four years. That's a whole lot of competitive spirit."

"Thanks, Dad, you have no idea how much I appreciate what you and Mom have done for me. There's no way I could have better parents."

Mom wiped away a tear, gave me a hug, and I headed for the dressing room.

When I went into the dressing room, the first guy I saw was Larry Bruce. Giving him a high five, I said, "That was a huge free-throw, Larry! You shot that the same way you do in practice every day."

Larry smiled. "I almost started walking to the other end of the floor on the outside of my ankles like we do in practice when I realized I had one more free-throw."

Now everyone was laughing. I said, "Listen, fellas. All those free throws that we shoot every day in practice just paid off. We made 14 of 18 free throws while they hit 10 of 18. We made four more free throws than they did and guess what? We won by four points."

James came up to me and shook my hand. "You remember two years ago at the state tournament I told you that we were coming back to state again before I graduate?"

With a big smile, I said, "Yes, I remember."

"Well, Coach, WE'RE GOING BACK TO AUSTIN!"

Now there was a high-spirited, very loud, positive response followed by a lot of fist pumping. As I looked around at the emotional happy faces in our jovial dressing room, I said, "It wasn't one of our more beautiful wins, but hey, a win is a win. We'll take it."

Jeff appeared to be feeling much better as he walked up to me and shook my hand.

"Coach, I've got something to say. I've been designated as the spokesman for this. Everyone knows that you have a birthday tomorrow and we want you to know that this win was an early birthday present just for you. Happy birthday, Coach."

I was a little misty-eyed when I said, "Thank you, fellas. You couldn't have given me a better present. I love you guys. Now, let's just enjoy this win."

With that, the hand clapping and cheering started all over again. When it died down, soft-spoken Carl Watson said, "We'd sing happy birthday to you, but I don't think any of us can carry a tune!"

Now everyone was laughing! There's nothing like that emotional happy feeling in the dressing room after a huge win, particularly when it sends you to the state tournament. Without me bringing it up, I think our team realized that we'd just dodged a bullet and won a game that could've ended our season.

As I walked out of the dressing room, I reminded myself what one of my fellow students in a coaching class at Sam Houston State University once said. "Really good teams that are well-prepared, although not always, usually win games that they probably should have lost."

We decided to stay and watch the Class AA final. Right before the game started, I walked down to the Diboll bench, shook hands with John, and wished him good luck.

"Go get 'em, Elliot Ness."

John's nervous expression changed to a slight smile and then a chuckle.

As I walked toward the stands, I looked back at him and said, "Hey, Kountze doesn't look near as mean as Al Capone. It should be a piece of cake."

The Pressing Champions

John had a slight smile on his face as I sat down in the bleachers. I'd hoped that I'd taken some of the nervous tension off John's mind because there's really nothing more nerve-wracking than the regional final.

There's really more pressure in the regional finals than anything at the state tournament because you have to win this game or there's no state tournament. Kountze was led by two outstanding juniors, Anthony Manning and James Branon. They also had an excellent coach in Willy Wilson.

Despite an outstanding effort by the Lumberjacks, Kountze won a highly competitive seesaw contest 59 to 57. I couldn't help but feel for John. It's really hard to take when you're so close and yet so far.

It was Sunday, March 1st. There was a slight chill in the air. It was my birthday and I spent the day with my family in Madisonville. Mom had asked me what I'd like for lunch after church and I requested her famous homemade stew. That's exactly what she made for me, along with some hot buttered cornbread. My younger brother, James Otis, looked at me.

"That was a great win considering the condition of some of your guys."

"Yeah, we hung on for dear life at the finish. It seems like every regional final goes right down to the wire. At least it's been that way with my three regional final games."

Mom's stew was absolutely delicious and I couldn't stop telling her.

"Thanks, Johnny. Be sure to save room for some cake."

Dad smiled and said, "I had a little input on the cake, son. I know you like pecans and I like coconut, so guess what, we have a delicious cake with coconut pecan icing. Happy birthday, son! We love you!

With a reciprocal feeling of love, I said, "Thank you!" and then took a bite of cake.

"Wow, Mom! This cake is delicious!"

It was great to be home and get away from all the hoopla of the regional tournament. I've always felt that I was blessed in having two extra special, loving parents and two great brothers. My family was exceptionally close-knit and I always knew that I had their total and complete backing.

My drive through the pines to school on Monday morning was one of both relief and satisfaction. When you're undefeated and headed for the playoffs, I found out that there's a whole lot more pressure on you than if you'd lost a game or two along the way. I knew this before the playoffs started, but it turned out to be much more pressure than I ever dreamed of. So far, we've survived and met the challenge. The question now is can we play well enough and win two more games? The great thing about those upcoming games is that they're going to be at the state tournament.

The Pressing Champions

As I pulled into the parking lot, while listening to the end of the news, I heard those famous last four words from my favorite news program: "PAUL HARVEY...GOOD DAY!"

Chapter 33

State Tournament Again

I was met at the steps entering the school by Emmit Roach, our principal.

"Good morning, Coach, and congratulations!"

"Thanks."

"Man, you gave us a scare!"

"Gave YOU a scare! I promise you that was not on purpose."

"Coach, I got a heads-up call a few minutes ago from Austin. They said to expect a call in 10 to 15 minutes, so why don't you go to the cafeteria, get yourself a cup of coffee and bring it down to my office?"

Ten minutes later, I was informed that we would play the Deweyville Pirates at 8:45 a.m. on Saturday morning and the finals would be at 8:30 p.m. in the evening. Class AA and AAA had their first-round games on Friday with the finals on Saturday.

I was disturbed by the fact that Class AA and AAA had a day in between the semi-finals and finals while our class had to play both of their games the same day. After all, we had four teams with a chance to win the Class A state championship. The two teams that played in the state final game should have the same amount of rest as everyone else so they can be at the top of their game. That's only fair. It's even more of a disadvantage when you run an all-out, highly aggressive full-court press the entire game. My team was in great shape and I constantly pushed them hard to maintain it.

Despite this, a second game in one day many times resulted in an ever-so-slight diminishing of physicality, particularly late in the game. I don't think my players realized this because I didn't bring it up, mainly for psychological reasons, but I did notice this to a degree in our regional final game. I planned on voicing my feelings on this once I got to Austin.

As I walked down the hall, I heard this voice behind me.

"Congratulations Coach!" When I turned around, it was Jan Blair.

"Thanks, Jan. Your cheerleaders did a great job Saturday night. I really appreciate all the backing that you girls did, not only Saturday, but for the whole season."

"Thanks. It means a lot that you appreciate what we do." As she walked away, she stopped, turned around, and looked back at me. "I just want to let you know that thanks to our cheerleaders your team is still..." then lowering her voice to a faint whisper, she said, "perfect." She smiled. "That's the way you wanted me to say it, right, Coach?"

I looked at her and said, "You said that perfectly!"

The next morning in the cafeteria, I was having a cup of coffee before school started. When Curtis walked in, I stood up and shook his hand. "I just want to thank you again for getting Donald to the game. You saved us. He played his heart out that first game and I know it took a lot out of him for the second game."

"I was glad to help out, Coach. I'm sorry that we didn't get there earlier."

"Well, it sure didn't have any effect on his play. That was one of his best games all year."

Benford then entered the cafeteria, took one look at me and said, "That was some kind of ball coaching Saturday night! What is it with you and these regional championship games? This is the third one I've been through with you. You won the first two by one point and Saturday night, with seconds left in the game, guess what, we're one point ahead!"

Now he was laughing "You just had to make it close, didn't you, Coach?"

I looked at him as I smiled. "Hey, I didn't want anybody to leave early. After all, we are in the entertainment business and I wanted every fan to get their money's worth."

Everybody was laughing as Miss Nona warmed up our coffee.

"Coach, what do you know about Deweyville?"

"We drew a mighty tough opponent."

"Teams don't make it to the state tournament unless they're really good, right Coach?"

"Right, Curtis, but this team appears to be exceptional. They have four guys averaging in double

The Pressing Champions

figures and two others at 9.6 and 9.7, so you might as well say they have six guys averaging in double figures. If that isn't enough to worry about, guess who they beat in the regional tournament? Friendswood, the team that we defeated in the state championship game two years ago and last year's state champion. I'm gonna tell you right now, they're gonna be hard to beat."

Curtis looked me straight in the eye. I'll tell you another team that's going to be hard to beat...The Kennard Tigers!"

The early part of this week, our practices were a tune-up of what we'd done the entire season. I purposely lightened the load because if we weren't in shape now, then we're never going to be. In essence, it was a review of everything that we did for the season, as well as a few new wrinkles that we might employ at the state tournament.

Donald had completely recovered and had his legs back underneath him. It's amazing what a day off and sleeping in your own bed can do for you. When you're about to go to the state basketball tournament, there's an anticipatory atmosphere of exuberance. This definitely showed in our short, but to-the-point practices as we prepared for a very tough opponent.

Deweyville was established in 1898 in far southeast Texas, about as close to Louisiana as you can get. This small town is located on the west bank of the Sabine River. This part of the state has long been a hotbed of

Coach Johnny Carter

high school basketball. Many state champions in the past have come from this area.

In reality, Deweyville was similar to our team as they had major contributions from all of their players. When you have as many guys that score as they do, I knew we had our work cut out for us.

We were allowed a 30-minute shooting session at Gregory gym at 9:00 a.m. on Friday, the day before we played our first game. Many nostalgic memories floated through my mind as we went through our early-morning shoot around.

Only three of my players were on our state championship team of two years ago, Lester, James, and Jeff. Lester, far and away our most experienced player, was making his third trip to the state tournament in his four years of high school, which was quite an accomplishment. The rest of my team were making their first trip to the state tournament. My three freshmen—Lester Woods, George Steed, and Paul Lamb were impacted the most by the size of Gregory Gym.

As George scanned the gym from top to bottom, he looked at his two teammates and said, "Man I can't believe how big this place is!"

As I stood at midcourt watching my team, I felt a tap on my shoulder. I turned around and saw Leon Black, my former junior college coach and presently the head coach at the University of Texas.

"Well, Johnny, you're back here again after a year's absence. Congratulations!" He had a slight smile and a pleased look on his face. "This is getting to be a habit. You're doing something right. I am so proud of you."

"Thanks, Coach. We're pretty lucky."

"I think you're underestimating how much hard work you put into your coaching. Sure, there's a certain amount of luck involved in this business, but those that have a passion for what they do and give it their all create their own luck. When you bring your team up here three out of the four years that you've coached, that's a whole lot more than luck."

"Thanks, Coach. I appreciate that. After all, a lot of what I do came directly from you."

A pleased look emerged on his face as he shook my hand again. "Thanks, Johnny, and good luck tomorrow."

Having been here before and played early morning games, I was using the same technique that I'd used in the past. We went to bed early last night, had breakfast early this morning, and had a shoot-around about the same time we'd play our semi-final game the next day. Hopefully this approach, which was basically a walk-through for tomorrow, would lead to the same result as our previous years.

Leaving the gym after our shooting session, Lester looked at me and smiled. This soft-spoken leader of our team said, "Coach, it seems like we've done this before."

"Yeah, son, this is the third time that you and I have gone down this road together."

"So why change anything, right Coach?"

"Right."

With a sentimental look in his eyes, he said, "Playing for you has been very special. These last four years have been a blast. Thanks for being my coach."

"I need to be the one thanking you. You've had a special career and a great senior year. Now we're coming down the stretch. Let's see if we can end this thing on a high note!"

This very humble young man had a serious look on his face when he said, "We've come too far not to get it done now, Coach. Tomorrow will be my last two games and I plan on going out in style."

After supper, we had a short team meeting at the hotel. I was going over some last-minute instructions for the evening and for the next day.

"We have a big day tomorrow and here's the plan. I can't over-exaggerate how important a good night's sleep is. We have two important games tomorrow. The first one is at 8:45 a.m. I'm glad we play the first game because it will give us a little more rest than the two teams playing after us.

"We'll be eating a pre-game breakfast, just like today...very early tomorrow morning. Getting to bed when I tell you is the most important thing for you to do tonight. Playing two games of this importance on the same day is hard enough, but if you don't get your proper rest that could affect the outcome.

"Look, I know all of you have had a good time so far and you've enjoyed missing school, but we're not on vacation. We're on a mission and we have a job to do tomorrow. You don't want to look at yourself in the mirror down the road and say, 'If I'd listened to the coach, we might have won.' We've got a tough game tomorrow.

I've known about Deweyville for a long time. One of my college teammates, Alford Barbe, an assistant basketball coach at Stephen F. Austin State University, is from there. In fact, most of you know one of our Kennard residents, Larry McClain. His brother Bob, one of our former students, lives there. He'll probably be at the game and just might have mixed emotions. Deweyville is good, *real* good. In some respects, they remind me of you guys. You might as well say they have six guys averaging in double figures. What does that say to you, Carl?"

Surprised by being singled out, he said, "It means we've got to guard all of 'em."

Smiling, I looked right at Carl and then the rest of the team. "Good answer, son. That's exactly what we've got to do. Once again, we're facing a team that's bigger than we are. So, what's new? Their two post men, Gary Knight and Charles Wallace are in the 6-foot-3 range. After that, we match up with them pretty well. James Wilson is their guard and leading scorer. They'll rotate Bimbo Wilson, Larry Shepard, and Biff Coleman as their forwards. All of these guys can and will score.

"Look, our defense has carried us this entire season and tomorrow you're going to have to play the best defense that we've played all year long."

James looked at me and then at the rest of the team. "Then that's what we'll do, right guys?"

It was almost like James was leading the choir because he ignited an absolute positive response, exemplifying a resounding affirmation. It certainly appeared that everyone in the room was on the same page. Now, if we can just implement and execute that tomorrow morning.

We arrived at Gregory Gym a little over an hour prior to our semi-final game. I wanted to get some early-morning extra shooting prior to our regular game warm-up just to get our team re-acclimated to this gym. It was important for my team to be as comfortable about their surroundings as possible. After all, this gym was huge compared to the many small gyms we played in this year, which made depth-perception an issue. This extra shooting session was more psychological than physical and would be nothing strenuous, just spot shooting.

As we methodically went through continuous shooting, both from the field and at the foul line, I walked up to James. "How do you feel, son?"

"Great! I'm ready, Coach. This is the last day that I'll ever play high school basketball. I'm going to give it everything that I have and you know what, I'm going to enjoy every second."

I smiled as I walked away because I knew that he was going to do just that.

The Pressing Champions

After our spot-shooting session and my pre-game talk, we jogged on the floor to an arousing ovation from our loyal following. To avoid the expense of a hotel, mainly because they couldn't afford it, most of our fans had gotten up very early to make the three-hour drive to Austin. They had to have left shortly after 5 a.m. to make it here on time.

I walked by the score table and shook hands with long-time public-address announcer, Phil Ransopher. He looked at me, smiled, and said, "Back again, Coach? What's this, your third time to be up here? Congratulations."

"Thanks."

I walked over and shook hands with Reid Smith, Deweyville's excellent coach, who was watching his team start their warm-up.

"Congratulations, on your great year, Coach."

He looked at me and said, "You're the one who should be congratulated. Coming up here undefeated just doesn't happen very often."

I smiled when I said, "Yeah, but it doesn't mean a whole lot unless you win two games up here!"

Walking back to our bench, I looked at my team. They were just standing there with their mouths wide open, almost hypnotized as they watched Deweyville's synchronized fancy warm-up drill.

I walked up to Lester and in a perturbed voice said, "Are you guys going to warm up or watch them warm-up?"

Coach Johnny Carter

Lester smiled and looked me in the eye. "Aw, Coach, that's a nice warm-up drill, but you don't win games in the warm up. When the buzzer goes off, we're gonna get after their butt!"

The quick smile from me soon became a serious expression as I walked back to our bench thinking about what was about to transpire.

When the game started, both teams came out of the gate full throttle and if the early minutes were any indication, there would be a lot of points put on the board. They matched us basket for basket and at the end of the first quarter, we had a slim 19-18 lead. Both teams shot an exceptionally high percentage and it was definitely an offensive first quarter.

In the huddle, I said in a fiery tone of voice, "I told you this team was really good and they basically just beat the heck out of our defense! This is the first time that's happened since the first half of that last Diboll game! You waited 'til the second half to take control of that game! Don't wait 'til the second half to take control of this one! I expect to see you dig deeper defensively in the second quarter. We've got to get some stops and create some turnovers! You've got to take over this game and show them who's the boss RIGHT NOW!"

As the huddle broke, Lester, who normally was soft-spoken, spoke out very emotionally when he said, "Enough is enough! Let's take control of this game right now!"

The Pressing Champions

We approached the second quarter with fire in our eyes and we got full extension both offensively and defensively. James got a steal and scored on a driving lay-up. Despite our height disadvantage, Donald and Carl continued to get clutch rebounds. Our press created a turnover, resulting in an easy basket for Jeff. It was a complete turnaround and we totally took control, giving us a 44-30 lead at halftime. It took the heart out of the Pirates.

We continued our onslaught in the third quarter and when Lester hit a free-throw line jumper, we increased our lead to 20 points. To Deweyville's credit, they never gave up and made a slight comeback in the fourth quarter, but it was too little too late as we won going away 79 to 68. Lester led the way scoring 23, followed closely by James with 19, as my two senior leaders provided the spark, both offensively and defensively igniting this total team victory.

Don continued to play exceptional defense, rebounded very well, ran the floor like a deer and scored 14 points. Jeff had an overall very good game, dishing out a bunch of assists and scoring 12 points. Carl was our leading rebounder for the game while scoring 11 points as all five starters reached double figures. This was the kind of balance that I'd strived for with this team from day one and today's victory was a direct result of total team unity. Both teams shot well over 50% and we overcame the size disadvantage, winning the rebounding battle 37 to 31. We had just soundly defeated one of the best teams in the state and we were now just one win away from the state championship.

Scouting the next game with my two brothers and Curtis, we watched the Clarendon Broncos defeat Coach Brenton Hughes' Itasca Wampus Cats. Coach Hughes had played many a game in this gym when he was a standout player for the University of Texas. Our state final opponent was led by 6-foot-3 all-stater, Charles Louis, averaging almost 28 points a game. However, Jim Moore, Bennie Reese, Steve Adams, and Wayne Carter all contributed with four of the five starters averaging in double figures. Clarendon had made it to the state tournament last year and was on a mission to win it this year.

Coach Carl Irlbeck was the architect of this team, which had compiled an outstanding record of 27-2. It's only fitting that the upcoming classic confrontation for the state championship would now be played out by two teams having a combined states best record of 70-2. The Broncos had a distinct height advantage and would be a formidable opponent.

My brother Billy looked at me with a concerned look in his eyes. "Louis is an all-around, multi-talented athlete. We've got to hold him below his average and that won't be easy."

Curtis nodded as James Otis added, "Don't forget about the other guys. They can all score!"

The Pressing Champions

"These guys are really good and they're going to be hard to beat!" Curtis said, "But you'll figure out a way!" he said confidently.

After lunch, we spent the rest of the day off our feet, lounging around in the hotel. The phone rang in my room. It was my dad.

"First of all, congratulations again on that win this morning. Second, how are you gonna stop that big guy for Clarendon? He can win a game by himself."

"Well, Dad, size-wise we have nobody that can match up with him."

"Well, son, how many games have you won this year going against teams that were bigger than we are?"

"A bunch."

"Diboll had that big guy and you beat them three times!"

"I still think they're the best team we played all year."

"It's not so much about the size, but what's in the heart that matters and your team has the heart."

"Who would you put on him, Dad?"

"I think I'd put Donald on him. He's quick, he's aggressive, he's smart, but the most important thing is he's got the heart."

"You know something, Dad, you would've made a great coach."

I couldn't see the look on my dad's face, but the warmth in his heart came right through the phone.

Coach Johnny Carter

1969 Dr. Pepper bottle.
Illustration by my son, John Carter

Chapter 34
State Championship Game at Last!

The time between games moves at a snail's pace when you're about to go for the state championship. Trying to relax is a virtual impossibility because a million things are rushing through your mind. I poured myself a Dr. Pepper over ice, walked over and gazed out the window. It was a beautiful early March afternoon. So much was on my mind that I couldn't really enjoy the beauty of the landscape.

The phone rang. It was my good friend, Tommy Ferguson. He was all excited as he told me that his Chester team had just won their semi-final regional tournament game at San Marcos.

When I told him that we also had won our semi-final game, he got even more excited.

"Hey, Johnny, the dream is still alive for both of us! Wouldn't it be something if both of us won the state championship? That might be too much to ask. Two classmates, teammates, best of friends, from the same small school win the state championship the very same year."

"I can't think of anything better than that. You know if that happens, it just might be some kind of a record. First things first! We both gotta win tonight and you'll have to bring your team up here and win two next weekend. Too bad McGilvra didn't make it up here. Kountze just won the state championship this afternoon and they beat Diboll by only two points in the regional finals. Good luck tonight, Tommy. Your team is in my prayers."

Suddenly, there was a knock on my door. It was Donald.

"You wanted to see me, Coach?"

"Sit down, son. We've got some very important things to discuss for tonight's game, but before we do, I want to ask you how you felt about this morning's game?"

"I thought we had a very strong game. Everybody did their job. Our defense was a big key and it took them out of the game in the second quarter. I love playing for this team, it's one for all and all for one. Today's win was a direct result of total team hustle, but that's nothing new, Coach. it's been that way all year."

"I couldn't agree more with what you said, I just hope that it lasts for one more game."

"It will, Coach. Believe me, it will! Just like all year, we're going to give it everything we have."

Listening to Donald, I smiled as many positive thoughts were going through my mind. Looking at my undersized, but very quick post man, I said, "I've got a very big job for you tonight. This is by far your most important assignment for the year. I want you to guard the big guy. I know Louis is bigger than you, but the way I look at it, you're the guy for the job. Can you handle that, son?"

"I guess I'll have to, Coach."

"I don't want to put any extra pressure on you, son, because this guy is a great athlete. I think the outcome of this game may very well be in your hands. He's averaging about 28 points a game. I expect you to hold him much lower than that tonight. You do that and we're going to win this game. If you don't...well, I don't even want to think about that."

The Pressing Champions

"Coach, I'll do the job! I'm not gonna let that guy beat us by himself."

"Look, I don't care if you don't score a point, this is what your main job is tonight. I want you to be in this guy's grill. I want you to totally frustrate him. You're very good on defense, you've got quickness, you're smart, you're determined, but the main thing I'm talking about here is that I've got a lot of confidence in you doing the job."

"Thanks, Coach, I won't let you down."

I stood in front of my team in the dressing room before the state championship game. It was unusually quiet.

"Well, fellas, the journey is almost over. This has been one incredible season, but we've got one more game. Our opponent is an outstanding, well-coached team. They made it up here last year and got a taste of what it's like. Last year's season highly motivated them to come back up here and finish the job. They think this is their time. Well, I've got news for them. THIS IS OUR TIME!

"Look, the main reason that we're here right now is because of our defense. It's been there all year and it's allowed us to overcome a lot of bigger teams and one more time that has to be what we do tonight.

Lester, how many games have we won this year?"

"42."

Coach Johnny Carter

I turned around, got a piece of chalk, and wrote a big 42 on the blackboard. I paused and looked into the eyes of every player on our team. I turned around and put a 1 right beside the 42. The blackboard now read "42-1." After letting that sink in for a few moments, I drew a big circle around it.

Now facing my team, I paused, pointed at what I'd written on the blackboard and asked in a fiery tone of voice, "IS THIS WHAT YOU WANT?"

There was a resounding "NO!"

Handing Lester an eraser and the piece of chalk, I said, "Fix it, Lester."

Lester immediately stood up, erased the board and put "43-0." He turned around, faced the team and shouted, "Let's do it!"

A few minutes later we had our prayer and headed for the court.

As I sat watching my team warm-up for the last time, my mind was reflecting back over the last four years. It had been like an extended fairytale. We were one game away from winning the state championship for the third time in my four years of coaching.

Clarendon, located about 60 miles east of Amarillo, in the panhandle near the Oklahoma border, had made it to the state tournament last year and was on a mission to win it this year. They were a very good team, hungry for a state championship.

The Pressing Champions

We definitely had our work cut out for us tonight because they had all the tools, plus they had the big guy, Charles Louis inside. Once again, we were going against a team that on paper looked to be a little better than us. In person, they definitely had a distinct size advantage. So far, we had managed to defeat every team we'd played that was bigger than we were. Hopefully, that would be the case again. It certainly didn't appear at the beginning of the game that our past successes against bigger teams would play out tonight. The Broncos appeared to be more like racehorses as they came out of the gate in full stride, stampeding their way to an early 9-4 lead.

My shell-shocked team was exploring unfamiliar territory because for the first time all year, an opponent dominated us from the start. Clarendon had a very talented team anyway, but now they had confidence seeping from their pores. Often a great start can propel a team to a great finish. We had a problem! With about four minutes left in the first quarter, I was about to call timeout to try and stop the bleeding. Calling a timeout early in the game was something that I rarely did, but in this case, it seemed to be necessary.

"Are you going to let these guys steal a state championship from you? Well, if you don't wake up, that's what they're about to do. They just slapped you in the face and made you like it. They have all the momentum right now. So, what are you gonna do about it? The first half of this quarter belonged to them. I'm telling you right now that the last four minutes of this quarter better belong to us!"

Before the huddle broke, Lester said, "We're better than this. Now let's go out there and show 'em that we are!"

We went back on the floor with renewed determination. After Lester hit a smooth 12-footer, capitalizing on his quickness, James stole the ball and scored. We soon regained the momentum and at the end of the first quarter, the score was tied.

The second-quarter went back-and-forth with the lead changing hands thirteen times and the score being tied six times. It looked like neither team was ever going to take control…that is, until 41 seconds were left in the first half.

Trailing by one point, Donald Denman hit 2 free throws, followed by a steal and a lay-up by Lester. Donald had been playing great defense on Charles Louis and on a missed shot got the rebound and rifled a quick outlet pass to Lester, who quickly drove the length of the floor. He then executed a fundamental crossover dribble, penetrated their defense, and with a quick flip of the wrist, launched a soft spinning free throw line jumper straight toward the rim.

Our crowd was soon rewarded when they heard the words echoing off the walls of Gregory Gym, "Basket by Lester Hutcherson!"

That last-minute surge which seemed to come out of nowhere put us up 35-30 at halftime, sending the

The Pressing Champions

Broncos to the dressing room with newfound doubt in their mind.

All year long I had stressed the fact that constant pressure defense many times can turn a game around in a matter of seconds. We had just scored six unanswered points in a flash and Clarendon could feel a major turning of the tide. That was the good news. The bad news was the halftime buzzer just sounded, giving the Broncos a much-needed reprieve.

I was certainly hoping the momentum that we had created at the end of the first half would carry over into the third quarter. *Would Clarendon utilize the halftime break to regain the momentum that they enjoyed at the beginning of the game? Would we come out flat to start the second half like we did to start the first half?*

I got my answer quickly because we took up right where we left off. James hit a jumper, followed by a Carl Watson tip in as we began to fan the flame. When James got a big steal and drove the length of the floor for a layup, it put us up 43 to 32 and we never looked back. Riding the crest of a phenomenal performance by Lester, we won the game 72-64, finishing the season undefeated, but more importantly, WE HAD JUST WON THE STATE CHAMPIONSHIP!

Undoubtedly, Clarendon's fans got real tired of hearing Phil Ransopher, the public-address announcer, repeatedly saying, "Basket by Lester Hutcherson."

Lester said he was going to go out in style, have fun in doing it, and that's exactly what he did and then some.

Displaying incredible determination, playing in his last high school game, this highly competitive young man put on one heck of a show, smoothly scoring a game high 33 points. He was virtually unstoppable in doubling his points per game scoring average.

Also playing in his final high school game, James popped the nets for 20 points, not to mention his game-changing hawking defense. While doing a great job on the boards, Carl was our only other player in double figures with 10.

However, the unsung hero in this game was Donald Denman. He had the unenviable special assignment of guarding Charles Louis. Donald more than accomplished his assigned mission, holding the much taller, all-state player to 17 points below his scoring average.

Dishing out assist after assist, just like he'd done all year, Jeff Myers once again used his point guard personality with precision in getting us over the top. We also won the rebounding battle over the much taller Broncos 48-41 as Carl, Donald, and Lester each got 12. Overall, this was definitely a TOTAL TEAM EFFORT.

Despite the disappointing loss, Clarendon gave it their all with four players in double figures as usual. Wayne Carter led them in scoring with 19, followed by Steve Adams with 14, Louis 11, and Bennie Reese, 10.

As the clock ticked off the waning seconds of this remarkable season, I glanced upward through the rafters of Gregory Gym, thanking the Good Lord for allowing me to be a part of all this. Before the clock ran out, the guys

The Pressing Champions

on the bench were congratulating me, as well as each other. When the final buzzer went off, the first guy to come to me off the floor was Lester.

Shaking my hand, he looked into my eyes and said, "That one's for you, Coach! Happy birthday again."

With a pleased smile, I said, "Thank you, son. You had one heck of a game! That's as good a state championship performance as I've ever seen! You saved your best for last."

"I just couldn't let those guys beat us, Coach."

As Lester and the rest of the guys lined up to shake hands with Clarendon's disappointed team, I turned to see my family right behind our bench. Mom gave me a Heart-filled hug, as did Dad. The look on their faces and the feeling in my heart said it all. Even though this was the third time for my family to experience this, it never gets old.

Billy looked at me with a happy smile on his face "I know you're big on total team play and that's what got you here, but you never know when that one guy will have the game of his life and that's what Lester did tonight. He was amazing!"

James Otis had a serious look on his face. "It's astonishing the mindset that you created with this team. Losing is just not in their vocabulary."

After shaking hands and congratulating Coach Irlbeck on his great season, we walked out to mid-court as our teams were lining up to receive their medals.

Phil Ransopher then announced to our highly partisan fans, "Ladies and gentlemen, let me introduce you to the 1970 undefeated Class A state champions."

We received an uplifting standing ovation as the celebration continued. When I walked in front of the score table, Phil stopped me. "You had asked me to get a score from the San Marcos regional. Where did you say your friend, Tommy Ferguson coaches?"

"Chester."

"I just got the score." He paused, then smiled real big. "Coach, I've got real good news for you. Chester won their game. They'll be up here next week going for a state championship."

I couldn't resist a couple of exuberant fist pumps. "Thank you, thank you, sir! I didn't think it would be possible to feel any better after winning this game, but you just gave me the best news that I could've heard right now. Thanks again, sir."

Although not knowing it at the time, Tommy would indeed bring his Chester Yellow Jackets to Austin the following weekend and win the Class B State Championship. I was thrilled for my good friend as he was absolutely awed by this experience. I don't know if this ever happened before. Two best friends, former classmates, teammates, and very fierce competitors from the same small school would win the state championship the very same year. Tommy and I were not the only ones in our 1961 class at Madisonville High School to make a career out of coaching. Kenneth Goodrum became an excellent track coach, winning two state championships. Between the three of us, we had six state championships.

As I walked back toward our bench, I was intercepted and hugged by our cheerleaders. Jan Blair said, "You didn't want me to say this before, but I can say it now. Your team was perfect!" She gave me a sly smile and asked, "And why were we perfect?"

"That's easy, with you girls backing us up, how could we lose?"

Our cheerleaders were all smiles as I headed back toward our bench where I was met by Curtis, Benford, and Miss Nona.

Curtis had a gleam in his eyes when he said, "This is far and away your best coaching job since you came to Kennard. Congratulations!"

Nona added, "This was one great year and I've enjoyed every second of it. You are one special coach. Thanks for coming to our little school."

"Thank you, Miss Nona for being our number one fan, not to mention making all of those great fried pies!"

Benford laughed and said, "You keep putting me to work. My shop class has to make another map for our already crowded gym wall, but you know what, I can't wait to get that done for you!"

I was smiling as I headed for our dressing room. Just before I went inside, I heard a voice behind me.

"Wait up, Johnny." It was Nelda. I immediately gave her a big hug and a kiss.

"Thanks for coming, it's great to see you."

"I haven't talked to you in a few days, but I know why."

"Yeah, I've been just a little busy the last few days. Man, you look great."

"Thanks. I appreciate that very much. Boy, your team played great today! In fact, they've done that all year long."

"Thanks. It's all about great effort and honestly, I've seen that from this team from day one. I know you're proud of Jeff. He did exactly what I asked of him and really was the glue that kept this team together.

"Man, I need to come back down to earth and I can't think of anyone I'd rather do that with than you. How about when we get back home I take you out for a nice dinner tomorrow night?"

"Sounds good to me. I'll see you tomorrow. You better get in there, your players are waiting."

Our dressing room was the epitome of youthful exuberance. All types of congratulatory gestures were made by the joyful victors. This amazing team had just gone 43–0 and in so doing, reached that elusive pinnacle of perfection. I was grinning ear to ear. I shook the hand of and hugged every player in the room.

The Pressing Champions

Lester looked at me with a gleam in his eye. "You remember what I told you last year after Alto beat us in the playoffs?" I smiled and nodded.

"I said that we weren't going to lose a game this year. WE DID IT!" Everyone cheered.

I looked at Lester and asked, "Did you really believe that we were going to go undefeated?"

He smiled. "All I knew was we had the potential to do that. When you work real hard, great things can happen!"

"Do you guys realize that Lester has been a part of three state championship teams and he's the only guy in this room that can say that?"

Lester looked at me and said, "Coach, there's one other guy in this room that has also done this."

"Who's that?"

Lester looked at me and said, "You left out the most important person on this team...YOU!"

That ignited a rousing ovation from everyone in the room.

Wiping away a tear, I said, "Thank you, fellas. I really appreciate that, but there's one other guy in this room that's also been a part of all this every year." I reached out and shook the hand of Clayton Baker, our manager.

"Thanks Clayton, you did a great job." Clayton smiled with his eyes, appreciating what I'd just said.

James reached out and shook Clayton's hand, then chimed in. "It's all about pressure defense, Coach. That's some kind of defense you taught us! Thanks for pushing us to play hard."

"Speaking of great defense, how about my man, Donald? You did some kind of a job on their big guy."

Donald smiled. "You told me if I didn't do a good job on him that we were probably gonna lose. I wasn't about to let that happen."

Donald then told me something that I'll never forget. "You know, Coach, as I stood out there at midcourt after the game, that was the happiest I've ever been, but at the same time, maybe the saddest I've ever been."

I looked puzzled, not understanding what he meant. Donald looked at me with mixed emotions when he said, "I was sad because I realized that the journey was over and Coach, I loved the journey."

I smiled and looked at Donald with compassion. "What just happened was what the journey was all about. Look, son, you and the rest of this team gave it all you had to achieve what we just accomplished. Every coach, every player, every team, as well as their fans, would love to be in our shoes right now. When that final buzzer went off, it marked the end of our season. This season just became a memory, but oh what a memory! All of you will be graduating one day and starting a new chapter of your life. You will always be able to look back on this day, this time, this team, and tell your kids, maybe your grandkids, just how special this day, this season was.

Jeff and Carl came by and shook my hand again. Jeff looked at me and said, "Thanks for being our coach. You inspired us to go way beyond what we thought was possible."

Soft-spoken Carl said, "Every day in practice and before every game, you made me feel like we were not going to lose and we didn't. Thanks, Coach."

Larry Bruce said, "I transferred to Kennard just so I could play for you. That's the best decision I've ever made. Thank you, Coach."

"Hey fellas, do you guys realize that if Larry hadn't made that free-throw last weekend in the regional finals that we'd probably be at home right now?"

Butch Jones said, "Let's hear it for my man, Larry!"

Larry was floored by the ovation he got.

Later, I was talking to the team for the last time.

"You know, before the season started a lot of people didn't think we had enough talent to come close to doing what we just did. Individual talent can win a lot of games, but if you don't play together, you hardly ever win championships. Togetherness and unity is what got us where we are right now. Every one of you accepted your assigned role and performed it pretty much to perfection. I knew after we'd played a few games that this team had a good chance to be special. You played the same way you practiced. It was all hustle, every second, every minute, every practice, every game. That's what it takes. Thank you for giving it all you had.

Coach Johnny Carter

"There's one more thing that you've got to do for me and for yourself too, before we get out of here. You have to promise me that when you say your prayers, you'll thank the Good Lord for allowing you to be a part of this special team. I love you guys. I will never forget this incredible perfect season."

**25-year Reunion of the 1970
Undefeated State Champions**
March 1995
Top (l-r) Lester Hutchinson, Jeff Myers, Butch Jones, Coach Carter
Bottom (l-r) Don Denman, Truman Lamb, Jimmy Twine, Rex Currie, Larry Bruce

The Pressing Champions

THE PERFECT SEASON: 1970

Kennard 82	Apple Springs 61
Kennard 66	Apple Springs 51
Kennard 38	Diboll 31
Kennard 72	Madisonville 44
Kennard 61	Diboll 52
Kennard 73	Neches 47
Kennard 63	Madisonville 31
Kennard 61	Chester 22
Kennard 69	Huntsville 35
Kennard 81	Iola 32
Kennard 69	Madisonville 47
Kennard 93	Lovelady 37
Kennard 82	Neches 38
Kennard 59	Lovelady 29
Kennard 71	Chester 56
Kennard 77	Lovelady 32
Kennard 59	A&M Cons JV 47
Kennard 81	Crockett 50
Kennard 74	Chester 49
Kennard 59	Iola 43
Kennard 86	Centerville (Groveton) 31
Kennard 80	Alief (Houston) 55
Kennard 73	Calvert 46
Kennard 65	Chester 43
Kennard 68	Iola 51
Kennard 67	Shepherd 36
Kennard 69	Diboll 61
Kennard 79	Iola 53
Kennard 42	Hudson 39
Kennard 68	Groveton 30
Kennard 81	Huntington 52

Coach Johnny Carter

Kennard 59	Central Cons 52
Kennard 49	Hudson 43
Kennard 80	Groveton 47
Kennard 68	Huntington 52
Kennard 75	Central Cons 68
Kennard 72	Alto 52
Kennard 60	Alto 56
Bi-DISTRICT	
Kennard 64	Troy 37
REGIONAL	
Kennard 75	Lexington 52
Kennard 54	Malakoff 50
STATE TOURNAMENT	
Kennard 79	Deweyville 68
Kennard 72	Clarendon 64

UNDEFEATED STATE CHAMPIONS
RECORD: 43-0

The Pressing Champions

1970 Undefeated Champions

(L-R front row): Don Denman, Carl Watson, Jeff Myers, Butch Jones, Lester Hutcherson, James Smith, Larry Bruce.

(L-R standing): Rex Currie, Johnny Burson, Lester Woods, Truman Lamb, Jimmy Twine, George Steed, Paul Lamb, Richard Curry, Bobby Woods, Clayton Baker, Coach Carter.

1970 TEAM

Coach Johnny Carter

Butch Jones

Carl Watson
1970 TEAM

The Pressing Champions

Don Denman

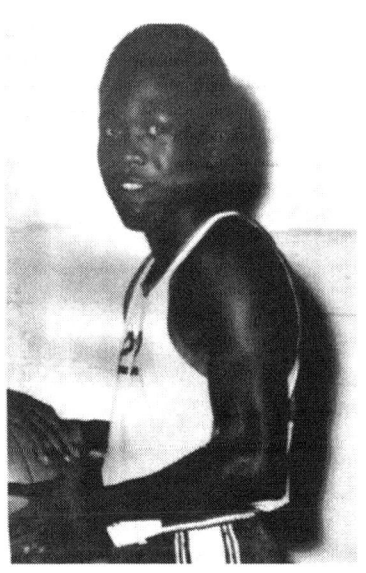

James Smith
1970 TEAM

Coach Johnny Carter

Jeff Myers

Larry Bruce
1970 TEAM

The Pressing Champions

Lester Hutcherson
1970 TEAM

Coach Johnny Carter

1970 Cheerleaders
(L-R) Betty Curry, Jan Blair (head cheerleader) Vicki Zalesky and Linda Wells (standing)

1970 CHEERLEADERS

The Pressing Champions

1970 Starting Five

Donald Denman: Our defense specialist
All tournament Centerville
Carl Watson: All District first team
All state
Jeff Myers: Our Assist Leader
All District, second team
Lester Hutcherson:
All District, All Regional, All State Tournament, All State
James Smith: All District, All Regional, All State Tournament, All State

Coach Johnny Carter

**1970 Starting Five with
1970 State Tournament trophy**

**Coach Carter with 1970
State Tournament trophy**

The Pressing Champions

Co-Captains Lester Hutcherson and James Smith hold 1970 state championship trophy.

Coach Johnny Carter

ONE SPECIAL MEMORY

Johnny Carter and the late Tommy Ferguson grew up together as lifelong friends. They are shown here shortly after both of their 1970 State Championship teams were honored at the 25-year State Tournament Reunion in 1995.

The Pressing Champions
CELEBRITIES

UCLA Coach John Wooden
Coach Carter 1976

Coach Wooden's teams won 10 NCAA championships the last 12 years of his illustrious Hall of Fame career.

Coach Johnny Carter

CELEBRITIES

Bill Russell, Coach Carter 1973
Bill Russell played 13 years with the Boston Celtics, winning 11 NBA championships during his incredible Hall of Fame career

CELEBRITIES

Coach Carter and Vinnie "The Microwave" Johnson
The Palace at Auburn Hills, Detroit, Michigan, 1994.
Detroit Pistons 1989, 1990.

"Coach Carter helped me bridge the gap from the playground to the NBA."

Vinnie played two years for Coach Carter at McLennan Community College and after finishing his college career at Baylor, he was the seventh player picked in the NBA draft. He played a huge role with the 1989 and 1990 back-to-back NBA champions. He is shown above with Coach Carter at a special ceremony when his number was retired. Vinnie is the third player in the history of the Detroit Pistons to have his number retired. The first two were Bob Lanier and Dave Bing.

Coach Johnny Carter

GREGORY GYM
Home of the State Championship Tournaments

Gregory Gym
University of Texas campus
Austin, TX

The Pressing Champions

University Interscholastic League 48th Annual Boys' Basketball
STATE CHAMPIONSHIP TOURNAMENT
CHAMPIONSHIP GAMES—GREGORY GYM

CONSOLATION GAMES—W. B. TRAVIS HIGH SCHOOL GYM

MARCH 7, 8, 9, 1968   AUSTIN, TEXAS

Official Program 25 cents

1968 State Championship Tournament Official Program

Coach Johnny Carter

1970 State Championship Tournament Official Program

ABOUT THE AUTHOR

Coach Johnny Carter was born and raised in Madisonville, Texas, and graduated from Madisonville High School in 1961. After an excellent basketball career at Madisonville, he went to Lon Morris Junior College on a scholarship. He graduated with a Bachelor of Science degree from the University of Houston and finished his master's degree at Sam Houston State University.

Coach Carter's first coaching job was at Kennard High School in 1967. In four years there, his teams compiled a record of 160-13, winning three State Championships in 1967, 1968, and 1970. The 1968 Kennard Tigers set three Texas State Tournament

Coach Johnny Carter

scoring records, the last of which—most points scored in a three-game series—still stands.

Carter served as an assistant coach at Howard Payne University in Brownwood, Texas for three years. They were the Lone Star Conference Tri-Champions in 1971 and played in the National AAU Tournament.

Carter was head coach at McLennan Community College in Waco, Texas, for seven years, finishing second in the conference in his first season in 1974. Thereafter, his teams won six consecutive conference championships. They qualified for the Regional Tournament every year, reaching the National Junior College Tournament in 1976. He was voted Junior College Coach of the Year by the Texas Association of Basketball Coaches that season.

In 1980, his team was the winner of the highest scoring game in the history of basketball: 169-165 against Kilgore. The game ball is in the trophy case at the National Basketball Hall of Fame in Springfield, Massachusetts. He coached two players at MCC who went on to the NBA: Vinnie ("The Microwave") Johnson and Sam Worthen. Vinnie, the seventh player taken in the draft, played on two NBA championship teams for the Detroit Pistons in 1989 and 1990. Sam was a second-round draft choice of the Chicago Bulls and works as a coach with the Harlem Globetrotters/Washington Generals.

The Pressing Champions

Coach Carter was an assistant coach at the University of Oklahoma for two years, reaching the NIT Final Four in 1982.

Carter was head coach for twenty-two years at Madisonville High School and had sixteen playoff teams. In 1995, they reached the State finals.

Throughout his career, Carter's teams were known for their aggressive full-court pressure defense, which he used every year after that memorable first season. His teams compiled an overall record of 903 wins and 241 losses.

Several of Coach Carter's players went on to have outstanding coaching careers. Among those are Danny Kaspar, Tony Mauldin, Eddie Nelson, and Randy Weisinger.

Though retired, Carter still works part-time for the Madisonville Consolidated School District and is also the play-by-play radio voice of Mustang Football and Basketball on KMVL AM/FM)

Watch Interview:
http://www.youtube.com/watch?v=hsDlx4whLxc
Visit my website: www.coachjohnnycarter.com

* * *

In May 2014, Coach Carter was honored at the Texas Association of Basketball Coaches convention in San Antonio, Texas when he was inducted into the Texas High School Basketball Hall of Fame.

Coach Johnny Carter

ACKNOWLEDGMENTS

To all the coaches who worked countless hours with me: Bob Ford, James Walker; George Autrey, Floyd Dickens, and Leon Black—plus all the others too numerous to mention whom I visited or listened to at coaching clinics.

To all the players I played with and against—in particular, the other four starters my senior year at Madisonville High School: Tommy Poe, Tommy Ferguson, Charles Grizzle, and Kenneth Standly.

To all the teachers, administrators, cafeteria workers, cheerleaders, and all those wonderful fans at Kennard who helped carry us through each season, especially the Harley Myers family. Mrs. Myers was like a second mom, having me over for dinner countless numbers of times.

To Bob Currie, a devoted fan and friend.

To all the student athletes who played for me in my 40-plus years of coaching. In particular, the Kennard players who accepted the big change I made in going to full-court pressure defense. They tirelessly worked with unselfish togetherness, establishing a great tradition that made my four years there a sheer pleasure.

To all the coaches, teachers, and administrators with whom I worked at Howard Payne University, McLennan

The Pressing Champions

Community College, University of Oklahoma, and Madisonville High School.

To Craig Smoak, a player, tremendous recruiter, and friend forever.

To the late Landon Holmon, thanks again for your help with the Bible verses in my first book. This young man's everlasting memory had a tremendous influence on my life, as well as others who got to know him.

To the late Johnny Wooden, who spent an entire day out of his very busy schedule to counsel a very inexperienced coach on the finer points of coaching.

To Robert Jones for his design and influence regarding the cover of this book.

To Susan Thompson for her time and talent in proofreading the original manuscript.

To all those who endorsed this book or took the time to read the original manuscript, thus providing some very appreciated comments.

To Carol Zimmerman for all her help with preparing this book for publication.

To Dorothy Hardy for re-making the cover. It's perfect!

To Jan Blair Felcoff for all her help.

Coach Johnny Carter

A special thank you for Cecelia Price, Kelly Moore, and Matthew Lupo of Carter Enterprises for all their assistance.

Thanks for all of the kind comments from the many people who read *The First Season,* thus making my first book a success. I greatly appreciate the encouragement I received to write this book.

Last, but certainly, not least, to my son, John, for all the special artwork. His detailed illustrations depicting various scenes and memorabilia added so much to the book. Thanks, son. I love you.

John Carter, Illustrator

The Pressing Champions

Praise for *The Pressing Champions*

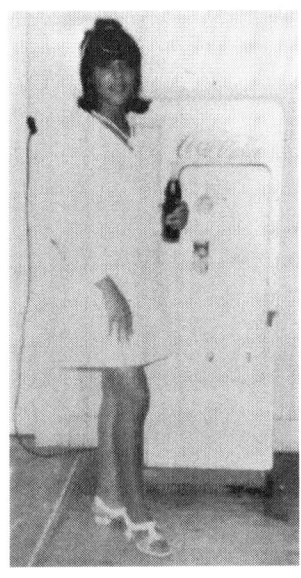

April 2, 2018
Dear Beloved Coach Carter,
*Donald gave me **The Pressing Champions** for my Birthday. Oh my, what a Gift! WOW!*

It's beautifully documented and written. Both volumes are masterpieces. After savoring every page, I feel 16 all over again! Your words about Donald and me are so gracious and kind.

*Your journals and records are envious and impeccable. It's so heartwarming to read how you revive, revisit, and cherish each life. But truly for me, this book is a **warm and passionate love story**.*

*Your Love comes through for Christ, for the Game and for People...people of each race, class and gender. On so many levels, **you told your story and "our" story!***

*Most of all, your presence and vision created extra ordinary experiences for a very special group of ordinary and gifted young black kids. At that moment and time, we could only imagine such dreams and notoriety (now, precious memories) were possible to witness and achieve at the **formerly segregated and newly integrated Kennard High**.*

Thank You, Love You...Our Great Coach and Visionary, Johnny Carter. May Christ Bless You and Those You Love, Always.

Most Sincerely, Debra Denman

Praise for *The Pressing Champions*

Jeff Wells, Senior Pastor
WoodsEdge Community Church
Spring, Texas

Johnny Carter gives us a page turner tale of basketball in a small East Texas town. But there is much more than just basketball here. Ultimately, this is the story of teamwork, determination, and a love relationship between a coach, a team, and a town. After reading this special book, I wish my son could've played for Coach Carter.

Other Books by Johnny Carter

Coach Johnny Carter

Made in the USA
Columbia, SC
02 June 2018